MW00427035

Ground Work

First Edition

LAYING

GROUND

A

WORK

FOUNDATION

ACKNOWLEDGMENTS

Thank you Christy, my best friend and beautiful wife, as well as Haley, Jonathan, and Aleah, my precious kids, for sharing your husband and father so selflessly with the work of the ministry. You guys are the joy of my heart.

Thank you, Lee Wilson for the hours you spent editing and rewriting my words, making them comprehensible. Thank you, Charlene, for sharing your husband's free time with me. Thank you, Thom and Elizabeth Wayne, for your additional work in editing this manuscript.

Thank you MaryAnne Hommel for reworking, rewriting, and reformatting this work and for the constant encouragement you and Dave are to my life.

Thank you, Eleazar for all the hours you spent formatting and designing this work, without you this project would have been impossible. I appreciate your friendship deeply and look forward to see all that God has for your life.

Thank you, Jesus, my Savior, my Friend and My King for continually being so merciful to me. Your grace in my life is completely undeserved but totally appreciated. It is an honor to serve You every single day.

PREFACE

First of all, I wanted to thank you for investing in this book and in your development in the Christian walk. I believe this book will help you understand some difficult things concerning the existence of God, the reliability of the Bible, and what the Bible says about our Lord.

I also wanted to make it clear this book is not written to be a scholarly textbook. Instead, it was written as an informative guide for the average church going Christian who sits in the pews each Sunday. As I wrote it I was picturing the precious men and women I have the great privilege of teaching week in and week out.

At the end of each chapter if I directly quoted a source, then that source is listed, however what normally follows is a "Further Reading" list from which you can grow in your understanding of the topic covered. I have listed books that have been a blessing to me and foundational in my personal understanding of God and His Word.

I also purposely wrote this book in the language I would use while teaching in the pulpit. It is meant to be conversational and again, not super academic. If I use theological terms, hopefully they are well defined and explained. The reason behind this is I have read many "scholarly' books in my day and sometimes they do a better job helping me sleep than anything else. I am thankful for the lifetime of study it takes to produce such informative works, but for me it often takes many ounces of Diet Coke to get through a chapter. I want you to enjoy reading this book. I want you to be able to finish reading this book and hopefully thereby grow in your relationship and understanding of our wonderfully amazing heavenly Father.

Pastor Jason Duff

TABLE OF CONTENTS

God
His Existence

WHY IS THE BIBLE A RELIABLE SOURCE TO LEARN ABOUT GOD?

"In the beginning God created the heavens and the earth."

Genesis 1:1

It is important that we understand what we believe about God. The apostle Peter said in I Peter 3:15, "Always be ready to give a defense to everyone who asks you a reason for the hope that is in you." We need to understand what we believe about God. As you can see from the verse above, it is also important that we understand why we believe what we believe about God. When we are questioned about our faith, the answer, "Well, this is what my parents believed," or "This is what my pastor believes," will not be enough. That type of secondhand theology probably will not even be enough to get you through your own crisis of faith that we all experience from time to time in this life. We need to understand what we believe, but we also must understand why we believe it. Conviction is important because that is what will help you walk through moments in your life where circumstances get you to question the reality of God's love in your life. We must have conviction; we must understand why we believe the things we believe.

"Ground Work" is a cool title (at least my media guys think so) for a study on the subject of theology. Theology basically means, "The study of God" and that is the purpose of this book. It would be impossible to put God under a microscope or take a DNA sample and learn what He is made of, but it is our desire to open up His Word and learn something about Him and hopefully about ourselves in the process.

Because it is so important for us to not only understand what we believe, but why we believe it, we need to start at the very beginning. If you are going to take the time to read this book about the study of God, then it is important that we lay the "Ground Work" for why we believe God exists in the first place. A belief in the existence of God is as foundational as you can possibly get, yet its importance cannot be overstated. For if your brain and heart cannot see the possibility of there being something out there greater than yourself, something we call "God", then there is no end to what you will believe in His place.

BELIEVING THE IMPOSSIBLE

Consider carefully this quote from George Wald, a biochemist from Harvard, taken from his article, "The Origin of Life". "When it comes to the origin of life there are only two possibilities, creation or spontaneous generation, there is no third way. Spontaneous generation was disproved 100 years ago, but that leads us to only one other conclusion, that of supernatural creation. We cannot accept that on philosophical grounds, therefore we choose to believe the impossible that life arose by chance." (Wald, P. 48)

By all accounts, if you are a biochemist from Harvard you are an incredibly smart individual. You don't believe that impossible things can happen. They are by definition . . . impossible. However, because Mr. Wald does not choose to see the possibility that there could be a God, then he is willing to believe the impossible. Believing in the existence of God is foundational to the rest of this book.

With the danger of coming close to quoting one of my favorite movies, "Nacho Libre", as you go through life you will be confronted by folks who believe that smart, thinking people believe in science, not God. They will say, "If you are intelligent, then you believe that we are here as a result of natural selection and natural processes, and if you are weak-minded, then you believe in God." Is that really true? Is the belief in God the same as believing in unicorns and fairies? I don't think so at all.

I believe there are good, rational reasons to believe that there is someone out there greater than you or me; someone who spoke this universe and everything in it into existence. The very first verse of the Bible states it this way, "In the beginning, God created the heavens and the earth." (Genesis 1:1) The Bible never seeks to defend the existence of God. The Bible assumes it should be self-evident, as you look at the world around you, that something out there greater than you exists. The skeptic asks, "Is there any evidence this is true? What signs would I look for if I wanted to build my conviction that God exists?"

THE SIGN OF DESIGN

There are many rational reasons to believe in God, but it is my desire to give you a few simple things to remember and hide in your heart to remind yourself and others you may be talking to about why it is rational, not crazy, to believe in God. I am purposely not using big words like the ontological argument or the teleological argument because I want you to be able to remember these things and use them in everyday conversation. Let's make it really simple - The first sign God exists is the sign of design.

Scientists get really excited when they find stone tools alongside human remains in a cave because it is evidence those humans intelligently put those tools together. The design that went into those tools is evidence there was a designer. No one would believe that Mount Rushmore with its carvings of four United States Presidents in the side of the mountain was the result of wind and rain erosion over millions of years. The intricacy of the design in those faces on Mount Rushmore screams that there was a designer.

Our world is full of evidence of design. Just a cursory study of the intricacies of the human eye, the DNA contained in every cell of our bodies, or the multiple factors that go into our blood's ability to clot, all have to be present in the original organism. These factors could not be added one step at a time over generations of species. You see these things and one can see evidence of a designer.

Even ardent atheists agree this world is full of evidences of design. Isaac Asimov wrote an article for the Smithsonian Journal titled, "In the game of energy and thermodynamics you can't break even." (This, by the way, sounds like a great summer read if you want to pick it up after you finish this book) Mr. Asimov wrote in that article, "In man there is a three-pound brain which, as far as we know, is the most complex and orderly arrangement of matter in the universe. It is much more complex than the most complicated computer ever built." (Asimov, P. 6)

Now, I agree, the human brain is far more complex that any computer man has ever designed. Yet I have a question for Mr. Asimov. If the human brain is far more complex than the most complicated computer ever designed, then doesn't it make sense that someone greater than ourselves must have designed our brains? No one would believe the computer I am typing on at the moment was the result of an explosion. No, someone much smarter than me designed this machine and wrote the software that it runs on. Design went into such a device, so it serves to reason that design went into the fingers, eyes, and thoughts that are operating the computer as well.

A DIFFERENT VIEW

Most people who don't believe in God will admit, "There appears to be design in the complexity of our bodies and the world around us, but the only real designer is small changes over great amounts of time." On the surface this seems to be a satisfactory answer. What looks like design is just the result of millions of small changes from the simple celled organisms of the past spread out over billions of years. It looks like design, but what you really are interpreting as design is one small change upon another over large amounts of time.

The theory sounds plausible because we all understand that natural selection is part of life. If a family of bunnies is running from a hungry coyote, then those bunnies who have slower genes and poor eating habits (with their little bunny tummies dragging along the ground) will become dinner for the coyotes. The faster bunnies will survive and pass their faster genes on to their offspring to produce a faster generation of rabbits. I have no doubt that is the way it works in the "natural" world.

Even though we observe the process of natural selection, the next generation of rabbits does not have any additional genetic information the previous generation did not possess. In order for natural selection to produce the evidence of design, it would have to add new genetic information to the next generation. That is the only way the rabbit is ever going to turn into the coyote that is chasing it. New information is needed.

Now listen closely – there is no known process by which mutation and slow changes over time add genetic information to an animal. That is not just the opinion of this Bible teacher; it is the opinion of the experts. Consider the quote from Dr. Lee Spetner from Johns Hopkins University in his book, Not by Chance. "In all the study I have done I my career in life sciences, I have never found a mutation that added information. All mutations that have been studied on a molecular level turn out to reduce the genetic information and not increase it." (Spetner, P. 9)

"Well," some might say, "If Dr. Spetner wrote a book called, Not by Chance, then obviously he already believes in God; of course he is going to write that." Okay, consider this quote from Dr. Werner Gitt, the director and professor at the German Federal Institute of Physics and Technology taken from his book, In the Beginning Was Information. "Can new information originate through mutations? Although the idea is central in representations of evolution, mutations can only cause changes in existing information. There can be no increase in information, and in general, the results are injurious, not helpful. New blueprints for new functions or new organs cannot arise from mutations. Mutations cannot be the source of new information." (Gitt, P. 10)

If natural selection and mutations do not produce what we see as evidence of design, then there has to be another source. That evidence of design that we see in the entire world around us must have originally come from an intelligence far superior to ours. Critics would say, "Okay, where did that intelligence come from?" We could extrapolate that to infinity unless there was a source of infinite intelligence beyond our finite understanding and that is exactly what the Bible indicates when it says, "In the beginning God created the heavens and the earth" – Genesis 1:1.

THE SIGN OF THE UNIVERSE

The second way we can see a rational reason God exists is the sign of the universe. The universe is here, you can go outside at night and see the stars of the galaxies, and you can take a telescope and see the intricacies of stars and planets and solar systems. Have you ever thought about how the universe got here in the first place? There are really only three options: The universe has always existed, the universe created itself, or the universe was created.

HAS THE UNIVERSE ALWAYS EXISTED?

Most scientists alive today do not believe the universe has always existed. Numerous evidences from the field of astronomy such as: the Background Radiation Echo theory, the Second Law of Thermodynamics, and the Motion of the Galaxies theory overwhelmingly point to the fact that the universe actually began to exist a finite time ago in an event when all the physical space, time, matter and energy in the universe came into being.

Think about what I just said. The vast majority of scientists agree the universe had a moment when it all began which is exactly what the Bible says in Genesis 1:1, "In the beginning God created the heavens and the earth." Scientists may not believe God did the creating, but they believe there was a moment when the universe came into existence. They do not believe the universe has always existed.

Consider this quote from Stephen Hawking, the very popular and immensely respected astronomer from Cambridge University. "Almost everyone believes that the universe, and time itself, had a beginning." (Hawking, P. 20) If one of the greatest minds of our time believes the universe had a beginning, we can rule out option number one: The universe has not always existed.

DID THE UNIVERSE CREATE ITSELF?

Did the universe create itself? That is an absurd thought. The scientific law of energy and matter conservation states, "From nothing comes nothing." Before the universe existed it would not have been around to do the creating. Things do not create themselves; they do not pop into existence. Based on our knowledge of science, we can agree that it would be impossible for the universe to create itself.

There are only three ways the universe could have come into existence, and we have eliminated two of them. We agree that the universe had a beginning point. We also agree that it would be impossible for the universe to create itself. This leaves only one more option: The universe was created. Consider this quote from Charles Darwin, "Reason tells me of the extreme diffi-fi

culty or rather impossibility of conceiving this immense and wonderful universe, including man with his capability of looking far backwards and far into future, as the result of blind chance or necessity. When thus reflecting I feel compelled to look to a First Cause having an intelligent mind in some degree analogous to that of man; and I deserve to be called a Theist." (Flew, P. 106).

If I were looking for signs that something out there greater than me exists, I would look for the sign of design and we see that in the world all around us. I would look for the sign of the universe. Our study tells us that it has not always existed, and must have been created. The first two signs we have discussed (The sign of design, and the sign of the universe) are good to know. I believe you should have some reasons for your faith, but keep in mind that people who choose to not believe in God can endlessly debate these topics. Their conversation might go something like this:

"Oh, you think design is a sign, an evidence of God? No way, what looks like design is just little changes and adaptations over billions of years. I know Pastor Jason says there is no know way that mutations add genetic information, but it happened, so there has to be a way. We just haven't discovered it yet, but we will." "And the universe, well yes, we know it hasn't always existed, and it could not create itself, but created, no way! The elements that went into the big bang evolved from nothing just like everything else later in the evolutionary chain. It's simple!"

Unfortunately, we could keep arguing like that forever because we interpret the facts through our worldview, and that is why our third sign is so important. If I want to see and share with others some evidences, a few signs that something out there greater than me exists, I would look to the sign of design, I would look to the sign of the universe, but most importantly, I would look to the sign of suppressed truth.

THE SIGN OF SUPPRESSED TRUTH

You see, we can argue with people for years about the

existence of God. They will state their proofs that God doesn't exist, and you will counter with your proofs that He does. In reality, I believe you have a great advantage in talking with non-believers because they have suppressed the truth in their hearts, and that is another powerful sign that God exists.

Romans chapter one says, "For the wrath of God is revealed from heaven against all ungodliness and unrighteousness of men, who suppress the truth in unrighteousness, because what may be know of God is manifest in them, for God has shown it to them. For since the creation of the world His invisible attributes are clearly seen, being understood by the things that are made, even His eternal power and Godhead, so that they are without excuse," – Romans 1:18-20 (emphasis mine).

I believe what Romans chapter one is telling us is God has revealed Himself to everyone. Now others may have suppressed that truth. The longer they live without God, the easier it is to push the inward knowledge that God is real out of their minds, but nonetheless, it is in there somewhere. Personally, before I had a real relationship with God, I would have told anyone I was okay; I didn't need a religious crutch, but when I would lay my head on the pillow at night, I knew I wasn't right. I knew something was missing. I believe that knowledge exists deep inside the heart of every person.

Now again, this is an advantage to you who do believe in God. You can pray for that loved one who has suppressed their knowledge of God, that they would see the truth and respond to God's invitation in their hearts. I have said to people many times as I am witnessing to them, "You know deep down inside what I am saying is true, that God is real, and He loves you and you need him. You can say all you want, 'I don't' but we both know that is not true." I have said that to many people I have been sharing Christ with, and I have seen many times, sometimes weeks later, that person come back to me and say, "You know, you were right."

Is there any evidence that man has suppressed the truth? Why would I mention it as an evidence for the existence of God? The reason lies in the fact I believe this suppressed knowledge of God is in the heart of every person. It comes out on a regular basis in things most ardent atheists believe and know to be true. Our job is not necessarily to argue about the existence of God until the cows come home, but to help people discover what they have oppressed in their hearts.

What do I mean? Well, why do almost all of us agree certain things are wrong? Believer and unbeliever alike, when we witness someone walk into an elementary school and start shooting little kids you would be hard pressed to find anyone who doesn't find that revolting to their hearts. Have you ever considered why we all agree that is wrong?

You see, if all humans are just highly evolved chemical reactions, then why is it wrong to hurt little children? Is it wrong for baking soda to react with vinegar? Then why is it wrong for me (a chemical reaction) to hurt another chemical reaction? Is it wrong for the lion to kill the gazelle? It might not be pleasant to watch on TV, but is it wrong?

Almost all of us would say no, but why? The reason is there is something inside us that tells us we as humans are different from chemicals or animals. Where did that knowledge come from? I suggest to you it was put there by God. You may have suppressed it, but it is still there under the surface.

HOW DO WE KNOW RIGHT FROM WRONG?

Most of us believe in some kind of right and wrong. The atheist doesn't believe the Ten Commandments were given by God, but if you take his wallet and steal his money, then you are going to find that he is a big believer in commandment number eight. Why is it wrong to steal? Why does almost everyone, even thieves, know instinctively that stealing is wrong? I suggest to you it was put there by God. You may have suppressed the truth, but it is still there under the surface.

When push comes to shove, no one really believes that morality is subjective. We say "accepted morality" is whatever the majority of people agree upon. Hitler convinced the majority of Germans his plan for the world was right, but we look on it today and know it was wrong. People will say accepted morality is whatever makes the most people happy, but why is that the standard?

Again, if we are only chemical reactions or evolved animals, then why should I care about someone else's happiness? Now I have a reason to believe that and live that out, because the Bible tells us to do it. The Bible tells me to love my neighbor, to even love my enemy, and to do good to those who use me, but why do most of us know in our heart of hearts that it is the right thing to do as well. I suggest to you it was put there by God. You may have suppressed the truth, but it is still there under the surface.

You see, the Christian world view not only accounts for morality, for why we know in our hearts that certain things are wrong, but the Bible also accounts for why atheists behave the way they do. Why they have a morality deep within their hearts as well. Romans chapter two tells us, "Even when Gentiles, (unbelievers) who do not have God's written law, show that they know His law when they instinctively obey it, even without having heard

it. They demonstrate that God's law is written in their hearts."
Romans 2:14-15 (New Living Translation)

The Bible tells us that the reason we know what is right and what is wrong is not because morality has evolved over time or because somehow we know that what is right is what is best for most people „ The Bible tells we know what is right and what is wrong because God has written His law on our hearts. We may have suppressed it, we may be running from it, but it is there, under the surface, and it colors so much of what we do, believe, and think. The morality in our hearts, suppressed but evident in many people, is another great sign that God exists.

ONE FINAL THOUGHT

Can I prove without a shadow of a doubt that there is a God? The honest answer is no. I can, however, give some good reasons that you are not the village idiot like those of us who believe in God are so often made to feel. I do not think it is just the "smart people" who believe in science while the "weak-minded" people believe in God, but at some point believing in God does require some faith. "Well, there it is," the atheist will say, "your belief is based on faith, my belief is based on science."

Wait a second, in reality both beliefs are based on faith. You remember George Wald, the biochemist from Harvard. He stated, "We cannot accept that (God created the world) on philosophical grounds; therefore, we choose to believe the impossible, that life arose by chance." Why would such a smart man believe that life arising by chance was impossible?

What is the chance that life arose spontaneously? Well, there are over 300 right-handed and left-handed amino acids (the building blocks of proteins and eventually life), but only twenty are used in the production of life. Those twenty have to be all left-handed amino acids, and they have to line up in the correct order of at least 100 in order to produce the basic building blocks of life. What are the chances that you would get the correct twenty left-handed amino acids to all line up in the correct order of 100?

Scientists have put the chances at the same ratio as flipping a coin and having it land on heads 100 times in a row. Now if you flip a coin the chances it would land on heads one time is 1:2, or every other time theoretically. What are the chances you would get heads 100 times in a row? You would have to flip that coin 300 million times a second for a quadrillion years to theoretically have it happen once.

Now think about that for a second. A quadrillion is a big number. Congress doesn't even deal with numbers that big. Naturalistic scientists tell us the earth is 6.5 billion years old. I believe it is much younger, but even if you give them that, it means there simply isn't enough time for life to have arisen by chance. If the same odds of life occurring by chance are the same as getting a coin to land on heads 100 times in a row, there just hasn't been enough time. Remember, it doesn't just have to happen once. You need a pink one and a blue one, and they need to find each other in the primordial soup and take in a nice dinner and a movie. This is why someone like George Wald would call life arising by chance "impossible".

My point is both the belief that life occurred spontaneously by chance and belief in God requires faith. If you want to believe that something happened that would require the same odds as flipping a coin 300 million times a second for a quadrillion years, you go right ahead. I have a much easier time believing, "In the beginning, God created the heavens and the earth." – Genesis 1:1.

Now how do know that the God that created this universe is the one we read about in the Bible? Why don't we believe in the god of the Quran or the god of the Hindu's Bhagavad Gita? What makes the Bible something we should trust? What makes it different than every other religious book? That is the subject of our next chapter, God – His Word.

WORKS CITED

Asimov, Isaac. *"In the Game of Energy and Thermodynamics, You Can't Break Even." Smithsonian Institute Journal. (1970): 6. Print.*

Gitt, Werner, Ph.D. *In the Beginning Was Information. Green Forest, AR: Master Books, 2006. Print.*

Hawking, Stephen, Ph.D. *The Nature of Space and Time. Princeton, NJ: Princeton Press, 1996. Print.*

Spetner, Lee, Ph.D. *Not by Chance. New York: Judaica Press, 1997. Print.*

Wald, George. "The Origin of Life." Scientific American. May 1954: 48. Print.

2

God
His Word

HOW DID THE BIBLE COME TO US?

"All Scripture is given by inspiration of God, and is profitable for doctrine, for reproof, for correction, for instruction in righteousness, that the man of God may be complete, thoroughly equipped for every good work."

II Timothy 3:16-17

We need to understand what we believe about God, and, even more importantly, why we believe it. Today, we need more than intellectual acceptance that God exists; we need conviction to get us through the trials and questions of this life. We are accomplishing this by laying a foundation for faith. In our last chapter, we laid the foundation for the existence of God. Now we need to move on to understanding why we should trust the Bible as a source of information to learn about God. Again, if we are going to spend time learning about God and ourselves from His Word, then we need the conviction that God's Word is a good source to use.

What makes the Bible different from other religious books? Why should we trust what the Bible has to say about God over what the Quran or the Hindu Vedas have to say? What makes the Bible different and trustworthy?

The Bible itself makes some pretty lofty claims concerning itself. Paul the apostle writes in 2 Timothy 3:16, "All Scripture is given by inspiration of God and is profitable for doctrine, for reproof, for correction, for instruction in righteousness, that the man of God may be complete, thoroughly equipped for every good work." Paul says all scripture, not some of it, or even most of it, is inspired. The word inspired means "God breathed." The Bible is claiming to be the very breath and word of God to us. This idea is becoming unpopular in some circles of Christianity today where they are teaching that the Bible contains or has some of the Word of God, or even becomes the Word of God once we believe it. The idea that the Bible simply contains the Word of God is far different than Paul's original statement that, "All scripture" is inspired.

The problem with taking the approach that some of the scripture is inspired, and not all of it, is that I have to become the judge of what is truly God's Word, and what is not. What would be basis of my judgement? Well, as I read the Bible, when I come to passages like this one found in Philippians, "My God shall supply all of your needs according to His riches." (Philippians 4:19) and I think, "Oh, I like that verse! That verse is inspired, that verse is really from God!"

Then I read what Paul said: "All who desire to live godly in Christ Jesus will suffer persecution." (2 Timothy 3:12) and I think, "Well, I don't like that verse. I don't want to suffer persecution. That verse must have been inserted in the text, it obviously is not inspired."

My emotions can't be the foundation for my judgement. When what I think or what I feel is driving my conclusions, I make the decision that suits me. I don't want to become the judge of the text, I want the text to judge me and my motives and my heart. I want to take the Word at face value and believe what the Word says about itself, "All scripture is inspired." Is there any evidence that this is true? Why should I trust that the Bible is any different than any other religious text?

The first reason to believe that the Bible is different from other religious writings and worthy of our respect and study is the process by which the Bible came to us. Have you ever considered what needed to happen to get God's Word from His heart to the Bibles we have sitting in our laps? I am going to completely over simplify the process, so this chapter won't get too lengthy (and I encourage you to do further study on your own), but you can remember the process by which God's Word came to us by remembering four steps.

GOD'S WORD CAME BY INSPIRATION

The first step in getting God's Word to us was inspiration. God put His Word into the hearts of men who wrote it down on papyrus, animal skins, and other writing materials of the day. How did that happen? Did the men lose control of their bodies and minds like they were possessed? I think a good source to answer what the inspiration process was like would be the Apostle Peter, who was obviously used to write inspired books. He would know what it felt like to be "inspired". He described the process this way,

"Prophecy never came by the will of man, but holy men of god spoke as they were moved by the Holy Spirit." (2 Peter 1:21)

Peter described "inspiration" as holy men of God speaking as the Holy Spirit moved them. That word "moved" is the same word another Biblical author, Luke, used to describe a ship being directed or moved by the wind. (Acts 27:15) It was not as if the sailors did nothing, or were in a trance. They lifted the sails, and they moved the rudder, but the direction and power was coming from a source beyond them.

God used each author's personality and life experiences to color the writings, but every word and thought and premise came from the heart of God Himself. It is these original thoughts from God's heart written by holy men of God that we claim are inspired (God breathed), inerrant (without error), and infallible (unfailingly accurate), for God does not err or lie.

The obvious question is how do we know that what God originally inspired men to write (which was without error and unfailingly accurate) is in any way close to what we have in our Bible today? That brings us to the second part in the process of God bringing His Word to us.

GOD'S WORD CAME BY DUPLICATION

After inspiration came the process of duplication, the process of copying those original documents inspired by God. In reference to what we call the Old Testament, ancient Jewish scholars gave their lives and careers to the task of copying the scriptures and ensuring it was without error.

One of these groups of scribes dedicated to making exact duplicates of the original scriptures was the Masoretes. These scholars were so committed to making sure their copies were exact, they would count every word of the Old Testament. In fact, they would count every letter. To check their work, they would count the letters knowing what the exact middle letter of the Torah should be, and if they were off by even a letter, all their work was to be burned and buried so whatever error they had made would not be passed on to the next copy.

When the text they were using to copy from had gotten old and faded, they would also burn and bury the old text to preserve the ability to make exact copies. Now, this burning and burying of worn and faded texts preserved the accuracy of what the Masoretes were copying, but it also means we do not have manuscripts of Hebrew text older than the 10th century. However, we can see their accuracy when we compare their text with older sources of the Old Testament.

The Greek versions of the Old Testament were called the Septuagint, named after supposed 70 scholars who translated the text from Hebrew to Greek. We have copies of the Septuagint from the second and third centuries and, compared to the Masoretic text, it matches perfectly. Another source used to compare the work of these ancient Hebrew scholars is the Dead Sea Scrolls, which were found in 1948 when a young Arab boy was looking for a lost goat. Along the way, the boy was entertaining himself by throwing rocks in the same way I have seen my own son do. One of the rocks went into a cave, and the boy heard the sound of pottery breaking. Out of curiosity, like any young boy, he entered the cave and discovered it was filled with pottery jars stuffed with ancient Hebrew writings.

Among the Dead Sea Scrolls was a copy of the book of Isaiah. When it was compared with the manuscripts scholars previously had that were written a thousand years later, they also matched perfectly. All of this speaks to the job the Hebrew scholars did in ensuring that what was copied was an exact replica of the original thoughts from the heart of God penned by men like Moses, David, and Isaiah.

DIFFERENT PROCESS, SAME RESULTS

Now what about the New Testament? The New Testament duplicators had no such tradition of burning and burying texts to ensure accuracy, therefore, we have literally thousands of manuscript copies of the New Testament by which to compare and check accuracy. We have over 5,700 verified manuscript copies of the New Testament as of the date of this writing, with more being discovered every year. Now, that number is astronomical when you compare it to other ancient books.

How about a quick comparison? Homer's Iliad, one of the most famous books of antiquity, comes in second to the New Testament with 700 manuscripts by which to check and verify its accuracy. There are only nine manuscript copies of Josephus and ten copies of Caesar's Gallic Wars. That means that most of what we "know" about that period of Roman and Jewish history comes from sources we can only verify from nineteen manuscripts. Compare that to the 5, 700 manuscripts of the New Testament.

The one downside to having so many manuscript copies of the New Testament is there are slight differences between the texts. That's what an educated Bible critic is talking about when he or she may say; "There are over 200,000 errors in the Bible." They are not errors, as in errors in doctrine, but differences in spelling of names and word order between the manuscripts. If one manuscript said, "Jesus went up the hill to meet James and John," and the next manuscript said, "Jon and James were up the hill, and Jesus went to meet them," the Bible critic would count that as at least three Bible "errors" because you have a different word order twice, plus a different spelling for John. In reality, you know exactly what happened no matter how you spell John or what order you arrange the events of the sentence.

We know and can verify the accuracy of 99.5 percent of the New Testament, and the .5 percent remaining has nothing to do with doctrine, teachings from Jesus, or salvation. It has to do with word order and the spelling of names. In fact, even if we didn't have the 5,700 manuscript copies of the New Testament, we could actually reconstruct the entire New Testament just from quotes contained in the writings of church fathers in the second and third centuries. You can rest assured that the Bible, both the Old and the New Testament we have today, is the inspired Word of God.

GOD'S WORD CAME BY CANONIZATION

The third step in the process of authenticating God's Word to us is called canonization. In the first century, like today, almost everyone writing a spiritual book claimed their book was from the Lord. Can you imagine today if every book in your local Christian bookstore was claiming to be inspired? The church needed a system to decide which books were really scripture, and which were not.

Now please do not think of the process of canonization as a group of robed men setting in a dark room saying, "I like that book but not that book." Thinking of canonization in those terms takes away from the ideas that all scripture is inspired. We must understand that most of what we have in our Bible was already agreed upon as scripture by the men and women who lived in the time in which it was written. In Deuteronomy 31, we see the writings of Moses laid beside the Ark of the Covenant as the people of that day realized what Moses had written was scripture. We see Daniel confirm that what his contemporary Jeremiah was writing was from the Lord in Daniel 9:1-2 (when compared with Jeremiah 25:11). In the New Testament, we see Peter confirm that what Paul the apostle was writing was from the Lord. Peter called it scripture. (2 Peter 3:15-16).

Most of what we have in our Bible was already clearly agreed upon as the Word of God. Some books like James and Hebrews that are in our Bible, and the Shepherd of Hermas, which is not, were up for debate. The early church fathers, with no doubt lots of prayer, put those disputed books to a series of questions. They asked questions like, "Was this book accepted by the early church?" Remember, many of the books of the New Testament were letters written to churches of the first century. Those churches would read and study those letters, and then pass them on to a nearby congregation. So the question was asked, "Was this book on the list of books read and studied by the early church?"

Then next question was, "Was this book written by someone who was a recognized leader in the early church and has that authorship been authenticated?" Many of the books that did not make it into the Bible and are instead located in what is called the "Apocrypha" which basically means, "writings in question" or the "Pseudepigrapha" which means "false writings". Many of those books were rejected because the authorship wasn't authenticated and verified.

Another question the church fathers would ask is, "Does this book align doctrinally with what we know for sure is scripture?" God is not the author of confusion (I Corinthians 14:33) and He does not change. The Gospel of Thomas 3:1-3, which in my opinion was rightfully rejected, records a story of Jesus as a boy killing another boy. Does that sound like the Jesus you know? Is that something the other trusted gospel sources just forgot to include in their account of Jesus' life?

If a disputed book passed this series of questions, then

the early church fathers included it in the New Testament as a scripture. Now to be perfectly honest, does this mean that every book God ever inspired is in the Bible? The honest answer is no; there may be a few books that fell through the cracks. What it does ensure in my mind is that every book that made it in was meant to be there, and I can trust it as inspired of the Lord.

GOD'S WORD CAME BY TRANSLATION

The final step in God's Word getting from His heart to our Bibles is translation. The Bible was originally written in Hebrew, Aramaic, or Greek. Until 1380, the only other language the Bible was available in, other than those, was Latin. That began to change with a man by the name of John Wycliffe, who wanted the Bible to be available in the common language of England. The church in Rome rejected this idea vehemently, even though that sounds crazy to our ears today. The Pope was so infuriated by Wycliffe's translation of the Bible into English that 44 years after Wycliffe had died, he ordered his bones to be dug up, crushed, and scattered in the river! However, the revolution could not be stopped.

William Tyndale holds the distinction of being the first man to ever print the New Testament in the English language. Tyndale was a true scholar and a genius. He was so fluent in all of the eight languages that he spoke that it was said you would think any one of them was his native tongue. Tyndale's translations of the Bible were burned as soon as the Bishop could confiscate them, but copies trickled through and actually ended up in the bedroom of King Henry VIII, which was probably the best thing to end up in the bedroom of King Henry VIII.

In the end, Tyndale was caught, betrayed by an Englishman that he thought was a friend. Tyndale was incarcerated for 500 days before he was strangled and burned at the stake in 1536, and his last words were, "Oh Lord, open the eyes of the King of England." This prayer would be answered just three years later in 1539 when King Henry VIII finally allowed, and even funded, the printing of an English Bible known as the "Great Bible".

After the death of King Henry's daughter, Queen Elizabeth, the version to end all other versions (or so they said) was authorized. King James I commissioned 50 scholars who took seven years considering the Greek and Hebrew manuscripts available to them at the time, plus the six English versions of the Bible to come before it, to produce the King James Bible. The KVJ as it's referred to today, was the gold standard of English translation for over 200 years.

Now, some people's devotion to the King James Version is almost cult-like. I have been told that the coming of the King

James Version was actually prophesied in the Old Testament. "The Words of the Lord are pure words, like silver tried in the furnace of earth, purified seven times." (Psalm 12:6) Remember, the King James Version was the seventh English translation, "purified seven times." I have had one guy even tell me, "If the King James was good enough for Jesus and Paul, it should be good enough for us." I find it ironic that in the attempt to be accurate, these statements could not be further from the truth! Today we have numerous great translations in English that can all be wonderfully helpful for Bible study. The English versions of the Bible today basically come from one of two types of Greek manuscripts.

TRANSLATIONS-WHAT'S THE DIFFERENCE?

The King James and the New King James versions come from a group of Greek manuscripts known as the Textus Receptus. All other versions come from older and more numerous manuscripts that were not available to the translators of the King James Bible, they are known as the Alexandrian Manuscripts.

Different from most of my contemporaries, I personally prefer the New King James Version when I read, teach, and study the bible. Using the New King James version as a Bible teacher today has fallen out of favor due to the fact that versions like the New International Version (NIV), New American Standard Version

(NASB) and the English Standard Version (ESV) are all based on manuscripts that are older and more numerous that those which were used to translate the King James, and eventually, the New King James Bibles.

Although I believe those versions of the Bible are wonderful translations, I am not so quick to throw out the New King James Version just because of the manuscript. You see, although it sounds counterintuitive to not go with manuscripts that are older and more numerous, those manuscripts that the NIV, NASB, and the ESV are based on come from the city of Alexandria, Egypt, hence the name, the Alexandrian manuscripts. Alexandria was known to be a hotbed for false teaching in the early church.

I personally wonder if the reason there are older and more copies of the Alexandrian manuscripts is because they are better, or because those early believers didn't trust them like they did the Textus Receptus? You see, if I have a favorite book, and I read it all the time, eventually that book is going to get worn out, and it will have to be replaced. A book that I never read and just sits on my shelf will eventually be older than the next copy of my favorite book, but the reason it is older is not because I preferred it, or because it was a better book, but actually quite the opposite.

I am not definitively saying that is how the early church felt about the Alexandrian manuscripts, because we have no evidence of how they felt about them one way or another. I just get bothered by the fact that if you use the King James or New King James Bible today, sometimes you are looked down upon for not using a "serious" version that is supported by older and more numerous manuscripts. I don't think we can be dogmatic one way or the other. The most important thing is that we read and study the Bible. I would encourage you to own as many versions of the Bible as you can. A real Bible scholar and great friend of mine once said to me, "You don't have to be a Greek or Hebrew scholar to understand what the Bible is 'really' saying in the original language. Just own five or six good different English translations."

We hear so often, "Well, it really says in the Greek . . .", but if men and women who gave their entire lives to understanding and translating Greek and Hebrew didn't translate it that way given five or six tries, then it probably doesn't "really" say that in the Greek as we so often hear.

Now we've dealt with the process of the Word of God going from the heart of God to the men who wrote it down, to the process of duplicating the text, canonizing the text, and eventually translating the text. I believe this is important because I find most men and women who attend church have no idea how the process took place. Next we'll deal with why we can or should trust the Bible as a reliable source on who God is.

FURTHER READING AND STUDY

- *"Evidence for the Bible parts 1 and 2" DVDs by Charlie Campbell – available through alwaysbeready.com*

- *"When Skeptics Ask" by Norman Geisler and Ronald Brooks – Baker Books*

- *"From God to us" by Norman Geisler – available on Amazon*

God

His Word (Part 2)

WHY IS THE BIBLE A RELIABLE SOURCE TO LEARN ABOUT GOD?

"All Scripture is given by inspiration of God, and is profitable for doctrine, for reproof, for correction, for instruction in righteousness, that the man of God may be complete, thoroughly equipped for every good work."

II Timothy 3:16-17

Is there any evidence that the Bible is really from God? The answer to that question is absolutely yes, and I credit my college pastor, (back when I was in college) and friend, Charlie Campbell for teaching me a simple way to remember the basic truths concerning the reliability of the scriptures.

Charlie Campbell is one of the greatest resources on the planet today when it comes to thinking critically about the Bible and his ministry, alwaysbeready.com is one you need to check out and be familiar with if you want to grow in your faith. Charlie uses the acronym FACES to teach an easy way to remember some ways to defend the validity of the scriptures, but when he taught my college group long ago, he used the acronym CAFES.

At a recent lunch with Charlie, I told him since he now uses FACES I was going to steal CAFES for myself. I remember Charlie used to tell us, "If they don't believe the Bible is the Word of God, take them to the CAFE and reason it out. So, what does CAFES stand for?

C-CONSISTENCY OF SCRIPTURE

People will say, "I don't believe in that book, the Bible," but I will always ask them which book? Which one? You see, the Bible is not just one book, but a collection of 66 books written by at least 40 authors, who lived in different times from each other. Paul, the apostle who wrote much of the New Testament lived almost 2,000 years after Moses wrote the first five books of the Bible. The Biblical authors lived at different times, they lived on different continents, and they did different things for a living. Some biblical authors were kings, some were shepherds, one was a doctor, one was a farmer; they couldn't be more different in their backgrounds. Yet even with all those differences, the Biblical authors agree from cover to cover on every controversial topic like, "What happens when I die?" "How do I get to Heaven?" "Is there a God, and what is He like?"

Now just imagine 40 people who live in your neighborhood, even 40 people who go to your church. You all live in the same basic generation, you all live in the same region of the world, and you even have a similar belief structure if they go to your church, but if I asked a series of controversial questions do you think they would all answer the exact same way? Questions like, "How do you feel about the President?" What is your stance on abortion in the case of rape or incest?" You would get a variety of answers from these people who have all had very similar life experiences. Yet the Bible agrees from cover to cover on every controversial subject and that is the first reason to believe its origin is from something beyond ourselves.

A-ARCHEOLOGICAL EVIDENCE

The "A" in CAFES stands for archeological evidence. We have evidence outside of the Bible itself that verifies the existence of at least 80 people mentioned in the Bible. Bible critics used to believe that Pontius Pilate, the man who convicted Jesus and passed sentence upon Him, was just a made-up figure, because there was no evidence of his life outside of the Bible. But in the year 1961 while digging in the sea side city of Caesarea, archeologists found a stone in the Roman theater with the inscription "Pontius Pilate, Prefect of Judea," showing not only did Pilate exist, but he was exactly who the Bible said he was.

It was as recent as 1991 that there was no evidence outside of the Bible that a man named King David existed or ruled in the Middle East, but that all changed when an inscription on a black basalt tablet was discovered just north of the sea of Galilee. It was written in Aramaic by Israel's enemies. They were bragging about defeating the Kings of Israel and the Kings of Judah, which they called the "Kings of the house of David."

Places in the Bible like Nineveh and biblical people like the Hittites used to be thought of as a fantasy have now all been verified by archeology as actual places and people. This is even more amazing when you consider that it is not true of any other religious book. Not one city, mountain, river, coin, or fragment of evidence has been found that supports the stories of the book of Mormon. Compare that with over 25,000 discoveries of people, places, coins, and writing fragments that verify the Bible is telling you a true account of history and archeology. This evidence becomes another reason to believe in the validity of the scriptures.

F-FULFILLED PROPHECY

There are 26 other books considered "religious", but not a single one contains any predictions of the future or prophecies that have ever been proven or verified as having been fulfilled. Contrast that with 27 percent of the Bible that was predictive prophecy at the time it was written. There are over 150 prophecies about Jesus coming to the earth the first time, and those prophecies were not things that He could make happen, like "Jesus will move to the suburbs in the fall."

No, the prophecies Jesus fulfilled had to do with where He would be born and how He would die. Fulfilled prophecy is a powerful argument for the scriptures having their origin in God, not man. Skeptics try to cast doubt on the biblical accounts and say, "Well, those prophecies were inserted after the time of Christ by His followers." The problem with that, however, is we have copies of the Old Testament that are dated before the time of Christ, meaning those prophecies were already in print long before Jesus lived them out. That fact alone makes it impossible that those prophecies were added to the Old Testament after the time of Christ.

How amazing is the evidence of fulfilled prophecy? In his now out of print book Science Speaks, Peter Stoner's peer reviewed research concluded that the chances of someone randomly fulfilling just eight prophecies in their lifetime to be 1 in 10 to the 28th power. Now that is a huge number.

To illustrate this, Stoner says the chances that anyone could randomly fulfill eight prophecies is the same as filling the state of Texas two feet deep with silver dollars, placing an "X" on just one of the silver dollars, blindfolding a man, having him walk anywhere in the state of Texas and have him reach down in that pile, two feet deep, and come up with the silver dollar with the "X" would be 1 in 10 to the 28th power.

That illustration is just for eight prophecies. Jesus fulfilled 150. There is no illustration we can conceive of to illustrate the idea this happened by chance. God, who knows the end from the beginning, was telling us the future in advance, proving to us, the Bible is not from the heart and mind of man, but the heart and mind of God.

E-EXTERNAL SOURCES

As we talked about with the proof of archeological evidence, so often people will accuse those trying to defend the Bible as "using the Bible to defend the Bible." We have many sources outside of the Bible that attest to the validity of scripture. Outside of archeological evidence, historians such as Josephus and Philo, who were not believers in Jesus, but Jewish and Roman historians, verify that the events we read about in the scriptures actually occurred. You may not yet believe in the God of the Bible, but the Bible is not a book of fairy tales. There was an ancient Jewish people, there was a man named Jesus who lived in the first century and died by crucifixion, and He did have followers who turned the world upside down. Those are undeniable, verified, historical facts.

S-SCIENTIFIC FACTS

The final evidence we want to cover is scientific facts included in the word of God. Even though the Bible was completed 1,500 years before the invention of the telescope or the microscope, the Bible contains no scientific errors. That is a miracle in itself when you realize the scientists who lived at the time of Moses and Job believed the world was located on the back of a turtle or Atlas, and if you sailed to the end of the ocean you would fall off. However, none of that ridiculous stuff is in the Bible. The Bible says, "He hangs the earth upon nothing. (Job 26:7)

Compare that with the Qur'an which states, concerning the sun, "When he reached the setting place of the sun, he found the sun sitting in a muddy spring" (Qur'an 18:86). Now what the Bible says about the sun is much different than, "It sets in a muddy spring." The Bible says, "The sun rising is from one end of heaven, and its circuit to the other end." (Psalm 19:6) For many years scientists said, "Everyone knows the sun revolves around the earth," or they believed the sun was stationary. Now we know it travels through space on a circuit at 600,000 miles an hour just like the Bible says.

In 1492, when Columbus sailed the ocean blue, many of his day said, "You are going to sail off the edge of the flat world." If they had just read their Bible, they would find that it says, "It is He who sits above the circle of the earth." (Isaiah 40:2)

People who want to get technical will say, "Well, the earth isn't really a circle." The Hebrew word used in Isaiah 40:22 literally means "sphere" which is exactly what the world is. The Bible is not a scientific textbook, but when it speaks on science, because the Bible is from the Lord, not man, it is unfailingly accurate; years before scientists understood the truth.

Before the invention of the telescope, scientists believed you could number the stars. The scholar, Hipparchus, taught in the schools of Greece one hundred years before Christ, "Everyone knows that there are 1,026 stars." The astronomer Ptolemy taught in the schools of Rome one hundred years after Christ, "We know there are 1,056 stars in the sky." Even the famous German astronomer, Kepler, said in 1630, "There are clearly 1,006 stars in the sky." The Bible states in the book of Jeremiah what we know to be true today, "The stars of heaven cannot be counted." (Jeremiah 33:22)

You see, people will argue today that while the Bible says in Genesis 1:1, "In the beginning God created the Heavens and the earth." science teaches us we have evolved, so you can't trust the Bible on scientific matters. My question is, "You mean the same guys who said there were 1,006 stars in the sky, and that the earth was swimming in an endless sea, the earth was flat, and the sun stood still or rotated around the earth. Do you mean those people?"

I am going to trust the source that has had everything right so far, no matter what the science of today may say. I believe the Bible is not from man, but from God. I believe one of the ways God proves that to us is to include facts about the earth and the universe, long before man ever discovered them. Those facts were written down at a time when the scientists of the day believed incredibly different things. The reason God did this was to prove to you the Bible is not from man, but from God.

TOTALLY UNIQUE

There is nothing like the Bible. That understanding affects our relationship with God. How? Because once we realize the Bible is from God, not man, then we are more apt to be given to the study of God's Word. It is once we are given to the study of God's Word that real change in our lives starts to take place.

The Bible says in the book of Psalms that the Word, "Makes wise the simple." (Psalm 19:7) David tells us the Word protects us from sin. "How can a young man cleanse his way? By taking heed according to your Word . . . Your Word I have hidden in my heart that I might not sin against you." (Psalm 119:9-11)

As Pastor Jon Courson is famous for saying, "Read your Bible and pray, every single day." It won't make God love you any more than He already does. It won't earn you favor or salvation from the Lord, but it will change you from the inside out which is what we all desperately need.

When I was a young man, my mother had this habit of

mouthing the words I was saying back to me when I was telling a story. She was so into the story, her mouth moved as if she was telling it. Being a disrespectful teenager, I would say to my mom, "Why are you moving your lips like that?"

She would say, "What are you talking about?"

"Your lips . . . they move while I am trying to talk!" Be careful what you say and do to your mom, because years later as a married man, I was sitting on the couch with my wife, and she was telling me all about her day when she stopped and said, "What are you doing with your mouth?"

I didn't need any explanation; I knew what she was talking about. I had become just like my mom. You see, the more we are around people, like it or not, you will take on some of their characteristics and quirks. Now that might be a good thing or not, depending on who you hang around!

When it comes to the Lord, there is no one I would rather be like. So spend time with Him, through the reading and believing of His Word. The Bible is not just another religious book; it is God's Word to you. The more I read it and let it read me, the more I begin to think like Him, act like Him, and see this world like He does because there is nothing like His Word!

FURTHER READING AND STUDY

- *"Evidence for the Bible parts 1 and 2" DVDs by Charlie Campbell – available through alwaysbeready.com*

- *"When Skeptics Ask" by Norman Geisler and Ronald Brooks – Baker Books*

- *"From God to us" by Norman Geisler – available on Amazon*

- *"The Fundamentals of Walking with God" by Jason Duff– (chapter 3 on the Bible) – available on Amazon*

God

The Trinity

WHY DO WE BELIEVE IN THE TRINITY AND WHY IS IT IMPORTANT?

"Hear, O Israel: The Lord our God, the Lord is one!"

Deuteronomy 6:4

We have discovered in our previous chapters that there are good intellectual reasons to believe that God exists. We saw in our last chapter that a reliable source to learn about God is the Bible.

Although there are 27 books man considers "religious" (The Quran, the Hindu Vedas, etc.), there is only one book whose truths are backed up by consistency of scripture, archeological evidence, fulfilled prophecy, and scientific facts. That book is the Bible, and when we open the Bible up, what does it teach us about this God?

One of the very first things we see about God is that He is a Trinity. He is one God that exists as three persons. Now I am well aware that is a simplistic definition, and true Bible scholars would feel the need to add and subtract words in my definition. However, I believe my definition expresses the basics of the doctrine of the Trinity. We believe in only one true God, but in the unity of the Godhead there are three coequal persons.

There have been very few doctrines that have caused as much confusion and debate as the doctrine of the Trinity. Sometimes I erroneously hear that the church in the fourth century invented the doctrine of the Trinity, and that it is not found anywhere in the Bible. That is completely untrue. The church councils like the Council of Nicaea in 325 AD were clarifying what the church believed since its inception. They were not inventing new doctrine, they were separating what was true and accepted doctrine from false teachings that were spreading throughout the church.

The doctrine of the Trinity was not invented by some fourth century church council, but is seen from cover to cover in the Word of God. It is seen in the very first verse of the Bible when God declares to us, "In the beginning, God created the heavens and the earth." (Genesis 1:1) The word the Lord picked to be used in that first verse of the Bible translated into English as "God" is the Hebrew word "Elohim". What is significant about that is Elohim is a plural word used for a singular God. We can see this truth later in Genesis chapter one when God uses plural pronouns to speak of Himself. "Then God said, 'Let Us make man in Our image, according to Our likeness.'" (Genesis 1:26)

The doctrine of the Trinity; however, is not based simply on the use of one word like "Elohim". The doctrine is based on the fact we see both the oneness of God, and the deity of God the Father, God the Son, and God the Holy Spirit all throughout the scripture. The word "Trinity" does not appear anywhere in the Bible, but of course the word "Bible" doesn't appear in the Bible either. However, the concept of "One God, three persons" is seen throughout the scriptures.

THE BIBLE STRESSES THE ONENESS OF GOD

The oneness of God was stressed in the great Hebrew Shema. Every Jewish child was made to memorize Deuteronomy 6:4, "Hear, O Israel: The Lord our God, the Lord is one!" The Old Testament taught the oneness of God and the New Testament would not disagree. Paul says in I Corinthians, "Therefore concerning the eating of things offered to idols, we know that an idol is nothing to the world, and that there is no other God but one." (I Corinthians 8:4)

Both the Old and the New Testament teach us clearly God is one, but both testaments also hint that there is more to this singular God than our puny human brains can grasp. Both the Old and the New Testament testify to the deity of God the Son and God the Holy Spirit.

In the book of Isaiah we are told, "Therefore the Lord Himself will give you a sign: Behold, the virgin shall conceive and bare a Son, and shall call His name Immanuel." (Isaiah 7:14) The word "Immanuel" means "God with us."

Two chapters later, Isaiah says again, "For unto us a Child is born, unto us a Son is given; and the government will be upon His shoulder. His name will be called Wonderful, Counselor, (and notice) Mighty God, Everlasting Father . . ." (Isaiah 9:6) The Old

Testament is clear, Messiah, Jesus, was going to be more than a great leader or teacher, He was going to be "Mighty God, Everlasting Father."

In the book of Micah, the Messiah is seen to be eternal just like we would think of God the Father. "But you, Bethlehem Ephrathah, though you are little among the thousands of Judah, Yet out of you shall come forth to Me. The One to be Ruler in Israel, Whose goings forth are from an old, from everlasting." (Micah 5:2)

THE DEITY OF JESUS CHRIST

The New Testament also teaches the deity of Jesus Christ, the Messiah. Paul says of Jesus, "For in Him (Jesus) dwells all the fullness of the Godhead bodily." (Colossians 2:9) Jesus, Himself, was pretty clear on the subject as well when He said in John 10, "I and my Father are One." (John 10:30) It doesn't seem like Jesus is confused on the subject.

THE DEITY OF THE HOLY SPIRIT

The New Testament also teaches the deity of the Spirit. Notice carefully Acts 5. "But Peter said, 'Ananias, why has Satan filled your heart to lie to the Holy Spirit and keep back part of the price of the land for yourself? While it remained, was it not your own?

And after it was sold, was it not in your own control? Why have you conceived this thing in your heart? You have not lied to men, but to God." (Acts 5: 3-4)

In verse three Peter is saying, you lied to the Holy Spirit, yet in verse four Peter says you were lying to God. Which was it? Was Ananias lying to God, or to the Spirit? The answer is both, because the Holy Spirit is God.

"Also I heard the voice of the Lord saying: Whom shall I send, and who will go for Us? Then I said, 'Here am I! Send me.' And He said, 'Go and tell this people: Keep on hearing, but do not understand, keep on seeing, but do not perceive.'" (Isaiah 6:8-9)   In Isaiah chapter six, Isaiah tells us the Lord said those things, but consider the Apostle Paul's quote of Isaiah in Acts chapter 28. "The Holy Spirit spoke rightly through Isaiah, the prophet to our fathers, saying, "Go to this people and say: Hearing you will hear, and shall not understand: And seeing you will see, and not perceive;" (Acts 28:25-26)

In Isaiah we are told, "The Lord said . . . ", but in Acts we are told, "The Holy Spirit spoke . . . ". Which one is it? Was it God, the Father who was speaking to Isaiah, or was it the Holy Spirit? The answer, of course, is both because they are one in the same. There is one God.

THE DISTINCTION BETWEEN THE FATHER, THE SON AND THE SPIRIT

The Bible, however, also recognizes a difference between God the Father, God the Son, and God the Holy Spirit. Matthew's gospel teaches us, "When He had been baptized, Jesus came up immediately from the water; and behold, the heavens were opened to Him, and He saw the Spirit of God descending like a dove and alighting upon Him. And suddenly a voice came from heaven, saying, "This is My beloved Son, in whom I am well pleased." (Matthew 3:16-17)

In Matthew, chapter three, we see this one God, but manifested as three persons. Jesus, God the Son, is in the water being baptized. God the Holy Spirit is descending in the form of a dove, and God the Father is speaking from heaven, "This is my beloved son . . ." The Bible teaches there is one God, yet at the same time the Bible teaches there is a distinction between God the Father, God the Son, and God the Holy Spirit.

We see this again in Matthew 28, "Go therefore, and make disciples of all nations, baptizing them in the name of the Father and the Son, and of the Holy Spirit." (Matthew 28:19)

We hear from the mouth of Jesus in His great commission that there is more than meets the eye to this "One God."

We see that same truth from the mouth of Paul the Apostle. "The grace of the Lord Jesus Christ, and the love of God, and the communion of the Holy Spirit be with you all. Amen." (II Corinthians 13:13) Paul, at the end of his second letter to the Corinthians, mentions the threefold nature of God. Remember, this was the same guy who wrote in I Corinthians chapter eight, "There is no other God but one."

We see it from the mouth of the Apostle Peter as well. "To the pilgrims of the Dispersion in Pontus, Galatia, Cappadocia, Asia, and the Bithynia, elect according to the foreknowledge of God the Father, in sanctification of the Spirit, for obedience and sprinkling of the blood of Jesus Christ;" (I Peter 1:2)

This doctrine of the Trinity is not just something Jesus came up with, or Paul the Apostle came up with, or especially not something the church came up with hundreds of years after Christ. The doctrine of the Trinity is something we see from cover to cover in the Word of God.

THE "WHY" OF THE TRINITY

I will be the first to admit that the idea of God as three but one is a very difficult thing for our minds to understand. However, I think it is one of the greatest pieces of evidence that the God of the Bible is not a God that man just made up. No one in their right mind, if they were making up the concept of God, would describe Him in such a "beyond our finding out" sort of way.

The Greeks and the Romans certainly invented gods, but their gods were just like them, only divine. The Greek and the Roman gods were lustful, bitter, and untrustworthy at times. In other words, they were just like the Roman and Greek people except that these made-up gods were all powerful and lived forever as the Roman and Greek people wanted to do.

It is only the God of the Bible that is altogether different than man. He is not like us in any way. Truly as the Word of God says about Him, "How unsearchable are His judgments and His ways past finding out!" (Romans 11:33) The doctrine of the Trinity is one of the greatest examples that the God of the Bible truly is beyond our finding out. He is not like me, only eternal and more powerful; God is completely different than you and me. He is not simply one, yet three. He is truly beyond our finding out, as we would expect a real God to be.

Now are there illustrations that can help our puny human brains grasp the Trinity concept of God? I have heard many in my life. Some find the illustration of the egg helpful. There is one egg, but the egg has a shell, a yoke and the egg white: so three, but one. The egg illustration can certainly be helpful, but at the same time it does not truly convey all that a Trinitarian God is. Of course if an egg could truly represent your god, in my opinion, that would not be a very good god to worship. With that said, the egg is not a perfect illustration because the shell of the egg is not anything like the yoke or the white in substance or makeup.

The opposite problem exists with the "role I play as a person" illustration. I am one person, but at the same time I am Jason the father, Jason the son, Jason the husband. The problem with this illustration is Jason the son is no different than Jason the father and there truly are distinctions between God the Father, God the Son, and God the Holy Spirit.

My favorite illustration of the Trinity is the three states of water. As you know, water can be a solid, a liquid, or a gas. I am told, however, that there is a scientific state of pressure and temperature know as the "triple point" where water can be a solid, a gas, and liquid all at the same time. If that is so, then the "triple point" for water is probably the best illustration we have in our world of the Trinity. The solid, liquid, and gas states of water make it distinct and different, but it is made up of the same exact elements, no matter what.

Beyond trying to make it easier for our human brains to figure out, it is also important to understand why the belief in the Trinity is important. When we come across doctrines that are hard for us to understand, the natural human tendency is to say,

"Well, this belief really doesn't matter." Nothing could be further from the truth.

Without the doctrine of Trinity interpreting some Old Testament passages becomes rather difficult if not impossible. One such example is in Exodus, chapter 3, where God tells Moses, "You cannot see My face; for no man shall see Me, and live." (Exodus 33:20)

In Numbers chapter 12 God says, "Hear now My words: If there is a prophet among you, I, the Lord, make Myself known to him in a vision, I speak to him in a dream. Not so with My servant Moses; He is faithful in all My house. I speak with him face to face, even plainly, and not in dark sayings. And he sees the form of the Lord." (Number 12:6-8)

How is it possible that in one place in the Word of God it plainly declares no one can see the face of God and live, yet in another part of the scripture it clearly says Moses saw the face of the Lord and lived? Is it a contradiction?

The same problem exists with Jacob in the book of Genesis, chapter 32. Jacob wrestles with God, then declares with some great surprise later in the chapter, "For I have seen God face to face, and my life is preserved." (Genesis 32:30) How are these things possible?

The answer is the Trinity. God the Father is that part of God that dwells in unapproachable light. God the Son is the part of God that puts on skin and interacts with man as we see with Jesus in the New Testament. God the Holy Spirit is that part of God that dwells within us, shaping who we are from the inside out. The scripture only makes sense, and is not contradictory with the doctrine of the Trinity.

The doctrine of the Trinity is also important for a proper understanding of what happened on the cross. I have heard the cross described as child abuse by God the Father pouring out His wrath upon His son. However, when we understand the Trinity, we are not dealing with three gods, one an abusive parent, and the other an abused child.

God is one, and the one God declared that sin: my sin and yours must be punished. On the cross it was the one God, yes, in the form of God the Son, who paid the price He required. It was not child abuse, it was not God passing the buck of sin, it was God taking on the punishment He declared must happen. This makes God totally just in that the righteous requirement for sin was paid. It also shows God to be totally love in taking my punishment on Himself.

FURTHER READING AND STUDY

- *"Basic Theology" by Charles Ryrie – available through Amazon*

- *"Systematic Theology" by Norman Geisler – available through Amazon*

God

The Father

"And the Lord passed before him and proclaimed, 'The Lord, the Lord God, merciful and gracious, long suffering, and abounding in goodness and truth, keeping mercy for thousands, forgiving iniquity and transgression and sin, by no means clearing the guilty, visiting the iniquity of the father's upon the children and the children's children to the third and the fourth generation.'"

Exodus 34:6-7

We have been laying the foundation of what we believe and why it is important. We have looked at good reasons to believe that there is something out there greater than ourselves, a God, who put this whole universe together. We have seen that the Bible is a very reliable source to learn about this God. In the Bible, God is described as a Trinity, He is one God that exists as three persons. The Bible teaches that there is only one true God, but in the unity of the Godhead there are three co-equal persons. Those persons are totally and completely God, but at the same time, there are distinctions. In this chapter, we will focus on learning about Go the Father. What is He like, and why is a right understanding of His character so important?

GOD THE FATHER

For some of us it is difficult to picture God as a Father. We live in a broken society where very few of us had great examples as fathers. Some of us have dads who are addicted to substances or were unfaithful to our families. Maybe you had a dad who abused you physically or emotionally. If you are in that place, when you hear that God is a Father, it is a hard concept to grasp because your earthly father has so many issues or was never there.

If you had a great dad, your dad was still a sinner, and

he could be inconsistent at times. I know I love my kids with all of my heart and I am determined to stay true to them and their mother in every way, but that does not mean I don't still have some glaring issues in my life... I do! Even if you have a great dad, the difference between your earthly father and God are so vast it is hard to picture God as a Father. How do we know what God the Father is like? The answer, of course, is in the Word of God.

The Word of God describes attributes of God, and those give us pictures of what He is like. Theologians call these "Perfections", and that term is used not just to sound fancy, but also to teach an important truth. God is the perfection of each of His attributes. God is not partly love, He is the perfect fulfillment of love. In everything He does, even in judgment, His love is seen. He is all that love is, and never what love is not. That is true of all of God's perfections, or attributes.

IT'S ALL IN THE NAME

The Bible lists hundreds of attributes or perfections of God, but I believe the best way to know what God is like, is to study the names God chooses to be called by in His Word. In the third chapter of Exodus, God was calling Moses to go back to Egypt to lead His people out of bondage. Moses said, "What is your name, who shall I tell the people sent me?" Understand, Moses was not asking that question just for information. He didn't ask for data about God, "God, I need your social security number, and your mother's maiden name." No, Moses asked the question for more than information. It was for revelation. He wanted to know who God was.

You see, when we ask for one another's name, it is for information. We want to go beyond calling each other 'bro" or "sis", so we ask a person for their name, for information. That is because in our society people receive names for many reasons, mainly superficial reasons. You received your name because your parents liked how it sounded with their last name, your brother's name, or it reminded them of someone in their past. The Jews however did not give names to their children for such superfi-
i
cial reasons. The names they were given were tied into who they were, their own personality.

So when Moses is asking for God's name, it is not for information. Moses knew it was God who was talking to him. I mean, whoever it was, was speaking through a bush! That is a pretty good indication you are dealing with something supernatural. Moses didn't want information for identification, but Moses wanted revelation. "I want to know who you are."

There are many names that man gives to God. "The Big Guy", "The Man Upstairs" or my personal favorite from Tommy Lasorda, "The Big Dodger in the sky." Even though that name is fairly close to the truth as every Dodger fan knows (What did God have David do to the Giants again?) we are obviously not going to look at those man-made names. Instead, we are going to look at what God chooses to call Himself so we might glean insight into who He is, and what characterizes the true and living God. There are four main names that God chooses to be known by in the Bible. There are many compounds of those four main names that teach us even more about the nature and character of God. Now let's look at the first one, along with some of those compounds.

YAHWEH OR JEHOVAH - "THE BECOMING ONE"

This is the name that God gave to Moses when Moses asked, "Who shall I say sent me?" It is also the most frequently used name for God in the Bible. Yahweh, as it is written in English basically means, "The Becoming One." That is seen a little bit in English when God's answer to Moses is, "I am who I am." (Exodus 3:14) God is telling us through His name that He will be everything we will ever need.

Jesus filled in the gaps a little bit during His life when He made statements like, "I am the door." (John 10:9) "I am the good shepherd." (John 10:14) "I am the resurrection and the life." (John 11:25) Whatever it is you need, the Lord will be that for you. We can go through life wondering how we are going to deal with this or that situation, and the answer is always the same. What we need is found in Him, in Yahweh, the great I AM. We see this even further in the compounds of the name Yahweh, or Jehovah in the scripture, further showing us how He is everything we will ever need.

JEHOVAH JIREH - "THE LORD WILL PROVIDE"

After Abraham obeyed God and was willing to offer his only son as a sacrifice, God stopped him and provided a lamb instead. It was then He revealed Himself for the first time as Jehovah Jireh, "the Lord will provide." (Genesis 22:14) This compound name of God teaches us that as we walk with Him and stick close to Him, God will provide everything we need. This doesn't teach that God will give you whatever you want. This name for God is often misused by those who teach what is called the "prosperity gospel." They teach the error that God will bless you (usually after you send them money) and give you whatever you ask for. God is not a cosmic genie, He is God who provides what we really need, and He knows best. What an encouraging thought!

JEHOVAH RAPHA - "THE LORD WHO HEALS"

Not only will God provide everything you need, but He is also the one who heals us. Primarily, I believe this is speaking of our sinful condition, and the curses sin brings to our lives. Healing represents the atonement Jesus gave us from the cross, but God also heals us of sickness and disease. God does not promise anywhere in His word to always heal us when we are sick; many times God is teaching us and others deep lessons through our physical trials. However, it never hurts to ask, and God's name has been honored many times as we come to Him to ask for healing.

JEHOVAH SHAMMAH - "THE LORD IS HERE"

Sometimes the enemy gets us to feel like we are all alone. Sometimes our sin makes us feel separated from God, but the reality in the truth of God's Word is He is always there. Theologians call it "omnipresent" and it means God is everywhere. This truth does not mean that God is in everything as the new age movement teaches. God is not in everything, but He is everywhere. How different we would live if we truly understood God is everywhere and sees everything.

When I was new on staff at Calvary Chapel Vista, I was walking down the hallway and I thought it would be funny to give our then youth pastor Scott Cunningham a quick "good game" pat on his backside. What I did not realize is the senior pastor was walking right behind me. After my dastardly deed, I felt a hand on my shoulder and a voice saying to me, "We don't do that kind of stuff around here." I was caught.

Now it's one thing when you are pulling a youthful stunt, it is quite another thing when we sin and live in rebellion and we think no one sees. The reality is, God is everywhere and sees everything, friend. That should be a great comfort to our lives when we feel alone. It also should be great motivation for us to think through where we are going, and what we are doing when we are in a time of rebellion.

JEHOVAH TSIDKENU - "THE LORD IS MY RIGHTEOUSNESS"

The final compound of Yahweh or Jehovah we want to consider is Jehovah Tsidkenu, which means, "The Lord is my righteousness". From this name I learn the important truth that God never intended me to approach Him on my own works and deeds. I need a savior. I need His righteousness applied to my life, and praise the Lord, He has provided the righteousness I need through the sacrifice of Jesus on the cross. Truly, God has given us everything we need.

THE NAME

In ancient Israel they had great respect for the name of God. They would never say it out loud, and they would never write it in totality. That is why we say Yahweh, or Jehovah. We really have no idea how to pronounce the name of God given in scripture, for the Jewish scribes would only write down the consonants "YHVH". When those scribes were reading the word and they came to "YHVH" they would simply say, "The Name". When they were copying the Bible they would take a ritual bath before they even wrote down the letters "YHVH. Now think about that when you consider this name for God appears 5,321 times in the Old Testament. That is over 100 times per book, and in some cases the name of God is used over ten times in one chapter. Now, that is one clean scribe!

It convicts me how lightly we take the name of God. Personally, I don't think God wanted them to have to take a bath every time they wrote down His name, but I do think every Christian should be careful of using God's name as an expression of fear or anger. For truly, His name is above every other name.

ELOHIM - "TO BE REVERED"

The second main name that God chooses to be called is "Elohim" and it means, "to be revered". Elohim is the first name God chose to be called in the very first verse of the Bible, "In the beginning God created the heavens and the earth." (Genesis 1:1) That word for God is "Elohim". Truly, God is to be honored and revered for He is so beyond us in every measurable way. Just as with Jehovah, there are many compound names of God using Elohim that teach us very significant things about His character.

EL ROI -"THE GOD WHO SEES"

When Hagar was cast out of Abraham's family and it appeared to her like no one noticed the injustice, God revealed Himself to her as "El Roi", "The God who sees". There is nothing that escapes His attention, which is the good news and the bad news. It is sobering to realize He sees all; there is nothing hidden from His sight. Again, theologians call this perfection of God, "omniscient", and it means "He knows everything." You can't hide things from God; He already knows. It does no good to put on a show, because God sees right through all of our religious facades. On the other hand, the fact that God is omniscient and still loves you is amazing news. I am convinced some people like me because they don't really know me, but that cannot be said of God. He knows every thought, every intent of the heart. He knows every secret that would make normal people run and scream from your presence, and get this, He loves you anyway. Great is the God we serve!

EL SHADDAI - "THE LORD ALMIGHTY"

What are you up against today? Isn't it amazing to know that there is nothing too hard for the Lord because He is the Lord Almighty? You are not going to face a problem where the Lord's response is, "Well, I have never faced that before. What are we going to do?" No way. When Nehemiah was up against incredible odds, he encouraged the people of his day to "Remember the Lord, great and mighty, and fight…" (Nehemiah 4:14) Sometimes, all that is needed when our back is against the wall is to remember who it is that holds our lives in His hands, El Shaddai, the Lord Almighty!

EL OLAM - "THE LORD EVERLASTING"

What a refreshing truth to remember the Lord is everlasting. He is not going to retire, quit, or get impeached. He is on the throne and will always be there. Even more, He always has been there. We can trust as God works in our lives that God knows what He is doing. We don't need to give Him the benefit of our insight, as I so often do in prayer. God has insight beyond what we can even imagine because He is eternal. We can have great faith and confidence because He is also unchanging. God doesn't have a bad day like we do or suddenly get an attitude as I can.

Growing up, I couldn't stand those teachers who were inconsistent. One day they would be happy, the next day they would be the Grim Reaper. One day homework was collected, the next day it was forgotten. I didn't like that because I didn't know what to expect. God is not like that at all. He is eternal, consistent, and totally trustworthy in our lives.

ADONAI – "LORD AND MASTER"

The third main name God chooses to be called in the scripture is "Adonai" which basically means "Lord" or "Master". This is another aspect of His character that I need to be reminded of constantly. In our Christian culture today, we often think of God as our brother and our friend. He is certainly those things, but we must never forget that He is also our lord and our commander.

I was reading through the book of I Timothy the other day, and I was struck how Paul "orders" Timothy to go places and take care of certain matters. I was thinking that wouldn't be received very well in our world today. We feel we have our rights and things that we deserve, but we have forgotten something very important and it's this; what we really deserve is Hell. What we really deserve is judgment from the throne of God for every wicked thing we have ever done.

Instead, what we have received is grace, but that grace comes with some responsibility. Paul said it this way, "For you were bought at a price; therefore glorify God in your body and in your spirit, which are God's." (I Corinthians 6:20) Paul had just been telling the Corinthians that they needed to deal seriously with some sin issues in their lives. Almost anticipating their response of "Why do we have to?" Paul says, because someone bought you. Jesus paid for you with His own blood and forgave you of your sins and freed you from eternal judgment. We like that part of the deal, but we forget that this transaction also makes Him our Lord. It is our job to obey the Lord and trust that he has our best interest always in His mind. Why would we believe anything else?

FATHER

The reason we can trust that God always has our best interest in mind is because the fourth and final name that God chose to be called by in the scriptures is "Father". One of the many things that sets God apart from all the other things called "god" in this world, God says, "I am your Father."

If you are not yet a parent, I don't think this concept impacts you as much as it will one day. I will never forget the first time I held my children in my arms. It was such an amazing experience because for the first time I truly felt unconditional love. Ever since that day, my love for them has never changed. I always want to bless them and lead them into what is best for them, even if they don't understand, because I am not just a friend or a buddy, I am their father.

1 John 4:8 says, "God is love." When we realize God loves us this way, it opens our eyes to what love truly is. He is everything love is, and nothing that love is not. That should change our view of His will, His Word, and the circumstances in our lives. We have the tendency to look at God's commandments and think, "Why is God trying to stop my joy?" That is the opposite of what is going on. God doesn't give His commandments because He was bored in Heaven and needed something to do so He decided to fill our lives with pointless rules. No, God knew certain things would bless us and certain things would bring pain, so in His love He tells us to avoid some things and run toward others.

FATHER KNOWS BEST

When we break His laws, He is not looking to strike us

down. That is not God the Father, but the "Godfather". When my kids were young, they had a fascination with putting things in light sockets. I would pull their hand away and the look they would give me, well, let's just say I'm glad babies are small because I think they would have killed me if they were bigger. They were sure I was stealing some joyous experience away from them. What they didn't know is the concept of electrical current and what they were attempting would not bless them, but instead, blast them.

My kids are growing up, and they are no longer tempted with light sockets. Now, a whole new list of rules have come to pass that at times, they don't understand. I get it because they are kids, but what about you and me? Do we believe our Father has our best interest in mind? Do we trust that as we follow Him, He will lead us into good things? If we struggle with this concept it is because we have forgotten that God is more than our master and our king; He is our Father.

I used to watch my cousins play baseball in little league, and my uncle, who at every Thanksgiving and Christmas was a normal mild-mannered human being, became something totally different at those games. He yelled and screamed, and, one time, I remember him clinging to the fence and just shaking it because he believed the umpire had made a bad call. What made him so passionate? Those were his kids.

I would watch that with an ounce of sadness because my Dad left our family when I was very young, and I wished I had someone who was passionate like that for me. I will never forget the day that the Lord whispered into my heart through His Word, "You do! I am a Father to you. I am passionate about you. I want the best for you, and you will walk in it as you follow my Word for your life." God will become everything we need. He is worthy of our respect and obedience, and He loves us like no one else ever will because He is our Father!

FURTHER READING AND STUDY

- *"Basic Theology" by Charles Ryrie – available through Amazon*

- *"Systematic Theology" by Norman Geisler – available through Amazon*

6

God
The Son

"For I delivered to you first of all that which I also received: that Christ died for our sins according to the Scriptures, and that He was buried, and that He rose again the third day according to the Scriptures"

I Corinthians 15:3-4

So far in our study of who God is, we've examined the evidence that shows there is someone out there greater than us. Next, we moved on to the next critical stage of understanding, the reliability of the Bible. We saw why the Bible is a trusted source to teach us about God, over every other religious book that is out there. Once we established the Bible is a reliable source, then we began to examine what the Bible says about God. We discovered that that He is a Trinity, He is one God who exists eternally as three persons.

The first part of the Trinity is God the Father, and in the last chapter we examined who He is by examining the names by which He chooses to be called. The Bible is full of the primary names of God: Yahweh, Jehovah, Elohim, Lord, and compound names of God such as Jehovah Jireh, "The Lord will provide."

We have now come to the name that is above all other names according to Philippians 2:9-10, Jesus! Jesus is another compound name for God because it means "Jehovah is Salvation." What an appropriate name for the Son of God who took our place on the cross. Now, I am getting ahead of myself a little bit, because before we examine what Jesus has done for us, we need to establish who Jesus is. Again, we do this from the perspective of the scriptures.

Some people wrongly assume that the story of Jesus

begins in the first chapters of the gospels. That is true when it comes to the physical man, Jesus, who was God made flesh and walked among us. However, the story of the Son of God, the second part of the Trinity, begins way before Matthew chapter one.

IN THE BEGINNING...

The statement that God the Father is eternal, meaning He had no beginning and He has always been, is equally true of Jesus. Jesus affirmed this when He prayed to His Father in Heaven, "And now, O Father, glorify Me together with Yourself, with the glory which I had with You before the world was." (John 17:5)

Before God ever spoke this world into existence, God the Father, God the Son, and God the Holy Spirit were together in that perfect fellowship of three, yet one, known as the Trinity. We see that Jesus was there at creation, actively participating in the process. "For by Him (Jesus) all things were created that are in heaven and that are on earth, visible and invisible, whether thrones or dominions or principalities or powers. All things were created through Him and for Him. And He is before all things, and in Him all things consist." (Colossians 1:16-17)

Jesus was active in the creation of the world. He was active in the history of the Old Testament. He did not take on the name of "Jesus" until He was born into this world, but in the Old

Testament, we see God the Son working clearly in the pages of scriptures. It is something that theologians call a "Christophany", an Old Testament appearance of Jesus Christ. When Jesus appears in the Old Testament narrative, He is a given a different title such as "The Angel of the Lord." We see Him appear to Hagar (Genesis 16), Abraham (Genesis 22), and Gideon (Judges 6) among many other places.

Now, some people have a problem understanding how Jesus be called an angel. We think of angels as little babies with wings or beings who are subservient to God. The Heavenly hosts we think of as angels certainly are lower than God, for they are created by God, but the word "angel" simply means "messenger". Often in the Old Testament, God would come, Himself to bring a message to His people.

One of the things that is confusing to some people about the Bible is that God clearly declares, "You cannot see My face; for no man shall see Me, and live." (Exodus 33:20) Yet Jacob wrestles with God (Genesis 32:30), and Moses talks to God face to face. (Numbers 12:7-8) How are those two things possible? Is it a contradiction in the Bible? No, it's the Trinity! God exists as God the Father, which is that part of God that no man can see and live. Jesus, God the Son, is that part of the Trinity that walks and talks, and sometimes wrestles with mankind.

Eventually that part of God, God the Son, took on our human flesh in something we call the incarnation. God the Son took on flesh and walked among us. This miracle happened through another miracle that is so often attacked by Bible critics. That miracle is something we call "the Virgin Birth."

THE VIRGIN BIRTH - HOW AND WHY?

We have heard the story and sung the songs every year at Christmas since we were kids, but how did the Virgin Birth happen, and why did Jesus need to be born into this world in this manner? "And the angel answered and said to her (Mary), "The Holy Spirit will come upon you, and the power of the Highest will overshadow you; therefore, also, that Holy One who is to be born will be called the Son of God." (Luke 1:35) The Holy Spirit, as the Bible says, overshadowed Mary, and she was with Child. Jesus came to this earth not through the normal means that you and I entered existence. He came to the world through no help of a man; He was put inside Mary by the power of the Holy Spirit.

This is not new information if you have been walking with God for a while, but have you ever considered why Jesus needed to be born of a virgin? Sometimes I think people believe it is because God thinks sex is dirty, and Jesus wanted a Mom who had nothing to do with that. Nothing could be further from the truth.

God invented sex, and He intends it to be a normal experience between a husband and his wife to produce children and grow closer to one another. Sex, the way God intended it to be, is not dirty at all.

The virgin birth came about for a completely different reason. Way back in the book of 2 Samuel 7, God promised David that eventually, through his sons, would come the Messiah. David was blown away that God would be so good to him and his family, but the problem was not all of David's sons were good guys. Many years later, one of David's descendants by the name of Jeconiah was especially evil. In Jeremiah 22:24-30 it tells us because of Jeconiah's great sin, God judged him and let him know that not only would he go into captivity, but none of his sons would ever again sit on the throne of Israel.

You and I might read that and think, "What's the big deal?" It was a huge deal and personally, I believe there was a party in hell when God spoke this to Jeconiah. You see, God had told David that through his descendants the Messiah would eventually come and rule over the nation of Israel. If none of Jeconiah's sons could be King, and the Messiah had not come on the scene at that point in history, then how would there ever be a Messiah? I bet the hordes of hell thought God had painted Himself into a corner. Through the Virgin Birth, we see that God is the master of the loophole.

When we get to the gospels in the New Testament some of you remember there are two different genealogies for Jesus. The first one is from chapter one of the gospel of Matthew, where we have the genealogy of Joseph, Jesus' stepfather. The genealogy in Matthew's gospel starts with Abraham and goes through David and through Jeconiah right to Joseph. Matthew was written to the Jews, and the point of that Gospel is to present Jesus as King over Israel. Jesus being the adopted son of Joseph has the legal right to the throne, even though that line was cursed by God in Jeremiah 22.

Luke's gospel also contains a genealogy of Jesus in the third chapter. Luke's genealogy goes all the way back to Adam, through Noah, through Abraham, through David, but instead of going through Solomon and onto Jeconiah as Matthew's gospel does, Luke follows Mary's genealogy to Jesus. She was a descendent of David's son Nathan, not Solomon; therefore, through her Jesus not only has the legal right from His stepfather to the throne of Israel passed down from father to son, but through Mary, Jesus has an uncursed bloodline to God's promise to David. Curses and our very sin nature, Bible scholars believe, are passed from generation to generation from fathers to their children.

By being born of a virgin, Jesus not only had an uncursed bloodline, but He also became the only man in history born without the curse of sin upon His life.

THE HYPOSTATIC UNION

God, the Son, becoming flesh and living among us is something the theologians call the "Hypostatic Union." This is a fancy term that simply means Jesus was both fully God, and fully man at the same time. This truth is hard to understand. How can anybody be 100 percent of two things? We can be 50/50, or 90/10, but not 100 percent of two different things. This truth is difficult to understand, but it is seen clearly in the scriptures.

The scripture teaches that Jesus was God. That truth is hotly debated today, and I have even heard some "authorities" on the Bible say Jesus never claimed to be God, and no one who lived during His lifetime ever considered Him to be God. Consider the overwhelming evidence from the Bible:

The Apostle Thomas knew Jesus was God:

- "And Thomas answered and said to Jesus, 'My Lord and my God!'" (John 20:28)

Isaiah the prophet knew Jesus would be God:

- "For unto us a Child is born, Unto us a Son is given; And the government will be upon His shoulder. And His name will be called Wonderful, Counselor, Mighty God, Everlasting Father, Prince of Peace." (Isaiah 9:6)

Paul knew that Jesus was God:

- "...Looking for the blessed hope and glorious appearing of our great God and Savior Jesus Christ." (Titus 2:13)

The Religious leaders knew who Jesus claimed to be:

- "Therefore the Jews sought all the more to kill Him, because He not only broke the Sabbath, but also said that God was His Father, making Himself equal with God." (John 5:18)

God the Father knew who Jesus was:

- "But to the Son He (God, the Father) says: "Your throne (Jesus), O God, is forever and ever; A scepter of righteousness is the scepter of Your kingdom." (Hebrews 1:8)

Jesus knew who He was:

- "I and My Father are one." (John 10:30)

- "Jesus said to them, 'Most assuredly, I say to you before Abraham was, I AM.'" (John 8:58)

JESUS WAS HUMAN

The scriptures are clear that Jesus was one hundred percent God, but at the same time the scriptures are also clear that Jesus was human. Many times the descriptions of Christ in the Bible demonstrate His humanity. "And when He had fasted forty days and forty nights, afterward He was hungry." (Matthew 4:2) We see Jesus thirsty in John 19, tired in John 4, and weeping in Luke 19. Jesus was fully God, yet at the same time He was fully man, experiencing the same human limitations that we do.

WHY DID GOD BECOME FLESH?

It is not something we think about much, but why did God take on flesh and become a man? I mean, if you think about it, God has been in heaven, being worshipped 24 hours a day, seven days a week for eternity. Why would He want to take on our flesh and live in this world with sickness and disease? Why would He allow Himself to become a baby and subject Himself to the care of sinful parents? I'm sure there are many reasons but I want you to consider three.

1. He came to reveal God to us

Jesus said, "He who has seen Me has seen the Father; Do you not believe that I am in the Father, and the Father in Me?"

(John 14:9-10) The writer of the book of Hebrews calls Jesus, "The express image of God." (Hebrews 1:3) This means that Jesus was like God the Father in every way. If you want to know what God is like, you simply need to get into the gospels and study and read about what Jesus was like. Look at the way Jesus lived, how Jesus felt about people and sin, and you will have a great idea of what God, the Father, is like. God became flesh in the form of Jesus to show us what He is like.

I once heard an illustration about a farmer who was having some doubts about the incarnation of God. He was wondering why God would go through all that trouble for mankind. It just didn't make sense to this farmer.

One cold winter night the farmer was watching a bird struggling against the cold. The compassionate farmer went out to his barn and opened it up and tried to push the bird in the direction of the barn to no avail. The bird didn't understand what he was trying to do, or the compassion he truly had in his heart for this little creature. The thought passed through the farmer's mind, "If only I could become a bird to communicate with the other bird, to show the bird the way and what my heart truly is for the bird, it would make things so much easier." Thinking on that truth, the farmer's heart was opened. "That is why God become a man." He became one of us to show us the way, to communicate the heart of God to man in a way that man could understand.

2. He became a Sympathetic High Priest

Another reason I believe God became a man was to be a sympathetic high priest. Jesus in His humanity experienced everything we experience except sin. He felt what it was like to be hurt, to be rejected, to lose loved ones, and to grieve. Why that is important for us to consider is that it changes the way we pray.

Hebrews 4:15-16 says, "For we do not have a High Priest who cannot sympathize with our weaknesses, but was in all points tempted as we are, yet without sin." Jesus became a man to know what it was like to face what we face. Imagine if, as a pastor, I never experienced any trials. You come into my office and start sharing with me about your broken heart over a relationship that didn't go as you had planned and my response was; "I don't know what that feels like; every girl I have ever known has fallen in love with me." What if someone died in your family and you came in for prayer and my response was, "Well, everyone I have ever known is alive and well." What if you were struggling with temptation, and when you came to me I let you know, "I have never been tempted in my life." I bet your response would be, "I want to see someone else; this guy has no clue what I am going through."

Sometimes we can feel that way as we cry out to God in prayer. "Do you now what I am feeling? Do you care, God?" The enemy lies to us and whispers in our ears that God is far away in Heaven, clueless to our human struggles, but that is not true. God became a human and faced what we face so we can come to Him in prayer and seek His Word for help, not from someone totally removed from life and troubles, but from someone who walked it all victoriously.

3. He came to win the battle we never could

The most important reason God took on flesh was to die in our place on a cross. You see, as we will study in a later chapter, sin requires the death of something innocent. The problem is, none of us are innocent; there is no way our good works or many prayers or even our own deaths could ever be the payment for sin. The battle against the penalty of sin was something we could never win on our own. Because of this, Jesus emptied Himself and became a man. Does that mean that He, for any time, stopped being God...no way!

Paul, the apostle said, "Let this mind be in you which was also in Christ Jesus, who being in the form of God, did not consider it robbery to be equal with God, but made Himself of no reputation... " (Philippians 2:5-7) Some have denied the deity of Christ by saying the phrase "made Himself of no reputation" means that Jesus emptied Himself, or stripped Himself of His deity; that Jesus was no longer God while on earth. This is a mis-understanding of the Greek language.

The phrase in English, "made Himself of no reputation" comes from the Greek work "kenosis". The idea of "kenosis" comes from Roman warfare. A centurion was the commander of 100 soldiers and a very skilled warrior. When the battle was fierce, he would strip himself of the markings of a centurion. He would then go to the front lines of the battle where the fighting was the fiercest. The word the ancients would use when the cen-turion would do such a thing was "kenosis". The centurion would remove the markings of his rank so he would not be singled out as the leader. He did not, at any time, lose the rank of centurion, but while stripped of the markings he would simply appear to be a normal soldier, and he would face everything a normal soldier would face.

Even though they looked like normal soldiers, it was clear that these men were not ordinary soldiers. These centurions would strip themselves of their markings and would come to the front lines because they were the only ones who could handle the job. They were the only ones suited for that difficult of a battle. Paul used this example to show us what Jesus did. God, the Son, became flesh and when He did, it was not that He stopped

GROUND WORK

being God. He never stopped being God. He simply looked like us, felt what we feel, faced what we face, and was still fully God. Jesus came to the front lines, stripped Himself of the outward markings of deity because He, like those centurions, was the only one who could get the job done.

Only Jesus never sinned. Only Jesus lived a totally pure and righteous life, and only Jesus then went to a cross to be treated as if He lived my life and made my sinful decisions. He did this so I could then be treated as if I had lived His life. It's the great exchange. Jesus came to die and He showed that He was who He said He was when He rose from the grave. The Resurrection is the last thing we need to consider in dealing with the subject of God, the Son.

HOW DO WE KNOW JESUS ROSE FROM THE GRAVE?

It sometimes surprises people to realize the fact that Jesus was without question a historical figure and not a mythological hero. Historians who lived during the first century, who were not believers in Jesus as God in any way, testify to His existence as historical fact. There are extra biblical accounts that there was a man named Jesus who was crucified by the Romans in Jerusalem, and this Jesus had followers who also went to their graves because of their belief that Jesus was God.

The historical evidence of Jesus also helps in discerning the truth of whether or not the resurrection of Jesus is a historical fact as well. The resurrection is really important because as Paul says, "If Christ is not risen, your faith is futile; you are still in your sins!" (I Corinthians 15:18) The resurrection, if it is true, proves that Jesus is who He said He was. If it is false, it makes everything Jesus ever did a sham. The importance cannot be overstated. How can we know for sure what happened in Israel so many years ago?

Remember, the fact that Jesus lived, died by crucifixion, and had disciples who also died for what they believed in, is a matter of historical fact. I am not saying that those historians believed Jesus was God, they did not; but they spoke to the absolute historicity of Jesus' life, death, disciples, and they way they died as well. Historians today believe that the disciples faked the resurrection, most likely by either stealing away the body of Jesus and then making up the stories we read in the Bible today.

The great problem with this view is the historical fact that Jesus had disciples who died for what they believed in. I can totally understand why people who had given their lives to follow a man, once they figured out He was not who they thought He was, would try to fake a resurrection to validate their lives. I get that. But remember, not only did the disciples all die for what they believed in, but many of them witnessed the tortuous deaths of their families. They witnessed the deaths of their wives and children without ever recanting their testimony that Jesus rose from the grave. Honestly think that through with me for a moment. People die all the time for what they believe to be true, but no one dies for what they know is a lie.

It is amazing to me that even knowing that the truth was Jesus actually rose from the dead, some of them still didn't recant their testimony while facing their own deaths and the deaths of their families. I don't understand how they did it, but the historical fact that they did teaches my heart one thing. Those disciples were not propagating a lie; they had seen something that Sunday morning in Israel. They had seen Jesus alive. The same disciples who abandoned Jesus as He was being crucified all died martyr's deaths because they had seen something that changed their lives. Jesus was alive!

I believe you can take that as a strong evidence for your own life that you are not dealing with a mythological god like the Greeks and the Romans worshipped. You believe in the true and living God who came to earth, and took on our flesh to die in our place. The God who will one day come again to take you and me to be with Him forever in Heaven.

The resurrection proves that everything Jesus said was

true and can be trusted. Jesus said, "I am the way, the truth, and the life, and no one comes to the Father, but by me." (John 14:6) Jesus said "I am the resurrection and the life. He who believes in me, though he may die, will live again." (John 11:25) Jesus is who He said He was. I believe that with all my heart. The question is, what do you believe? What you believe has consequences, and what you believe about who Jesus is has consequences into eternity.

FURTHER READING AND STUDY

- *"Basic Theology" by Charles Ryrie – available through Amazon*

- *"Systematic Theology" by Norman Geisler – available through Amazon*

- *"Evidence that Demands a Verdict" by Josh McDowell– available through Amazon*

- *"The case for the Resurrection" DVDs by Charlie Campbell – available through alwaysbeready.com*

7

God
The Holy Spirit

"And the Lord God formed man of the dust of the ground, and breathed into his nostrils the breath of life; and man became a living being."

Genesis 2:7

We have established that there is good evidence someone is out there greater than us, who designed us and brought this world and universe into existence. We have established that the Bible is a reliable source to learn about this "someone" who is greater than us. We learned that "someone" is God, and He is described as a Trinity. He is one God that exists eternally as three persons, God the Father, God the Son, and God the Holy Spirit.

We have now come to the third part of the trinity, God, the Holy Spirit. He is the often ignored or misunderstood person of the Trinity. A.W. Tozer said, "In most Christian churches the Spirit is entirely overlooked. Whether He is present or absent makes no real difference to anyone. Brief reference is made to Him in the Doxology and the Benediction, further than that, He might as well not exist. The idea of the Spirit held by the average church member is so vague as to be nearly nonexistent, and this has resulted in a distortion of Christian doctrine and an impoverishment of Christian life and work." After a statement like that we must ask ourselves, who is the Holy Spirit, and why is He important to our Christian lives?

WHO IS THE HOLY SPIRIT?

The first thing we need to understand is the Holy Spirit is not an "it", but a "He". So often we say things like, "I love the Holy

Spirit; I want more of 'it' in my life." This is completely misguided. The Holy Spirit is not a force or a special magical power, but a person. We see in scripture that the Holy Spirit can be grieved (Ephesians 4:30), has a will, (I Corinthians 12:11), can be lied to (Acts 5:3), and even performs miracles (Acts 8:39). These are not things a force or an "it" experiences. These are the characteristics of a person or a being.

It is important for us to understand that the Holy Spirit is not just a person; He is God in every way. Psalm 139:7 demonstrates that He is omnipresent; He is everywhere. Job 33:4 lets us see that the Holy Spirit is omnipotent; He is all powerful. These qualities we normally attribute to God, the Father, but they are equally true of God, the Holy Spirit.

God, the Father, God, the Son, and God, the Holy Spirit have the same characteristics, because they are one. Each part of the Trinity has a distinct role to play in the lives of mankind. God, the Father, so loved the world that He decided to redeem us by sending us His only Son. (John 3:16) God, the Son became flesh and dwelt among us and took our place on the cross. (John 1:14) God, the Holy Spirit has distinct roles as well.

WHAT IS THE PURPOSE OF THE HOLY SPIRIT?

We are told of at least four specific roles the Holy Spirit

has in our lives and in the world. The first role of the Holy Spirit is to convict the world of sin. Jesus said, concerning the first purpose of the Holy Spirit, "And when He has come, He will convict the world of sin, and of righteousness, and of judgment: of sin because they do not believe in Me;" (John 16:8-9)

The Holy Spirit's first job is to convict the world of sin. Think back to when you didn't know the Lord as your savior. You could put on a good show and smile and pretend like everything was okay, but deep in your heart, you knew you were not okay. You were under the conviction of the Holy Spirit. You may have called it your conscience or the little angel on your shoulder, but who it really was, was God, the Holy Spirit letting you know, "You are not okay; you need a savior."

HE IS THE PROMISE OF THINGS TO COME

The second ministry of the Holy Spirit in our lives is to provide evidence this relationship with God is real. Paul says it this way in Ephesians chapter one, "In Him you also trusted, after you heard the word of truth, the gospel of your salvation; in whom also, having believed, you were sealed with the Holy Spirit of promise, who is the guarantee of our inheritance until the redemption of the purchased possession, to the praise of His glory." (Ephesians 1:13-14)

The word for "sealed" in verse thirteen is closely related to the word from which we get the understanding of an engagement ring. A long time ago, some very smart women decided that if they were going to buy dresses and plan formal ceremonies called weddings and all the men had to do was dress nicely and invite a few friends, then they wanted rings. They wanted a promise that more was on the way.

The Holy Spirit is the promise from God that more is on the way. You see, after you give into the conviction of the Holy Spirit, the Spirit then begins to shape you and change you. I know we still have a long way to go, but praise the Lord we are not who we used to be. God, the Holy Spirit, has been slowly changing our language, our thought life, and our actions. Those slow changes are the evidence this relationship is real, and one day we will be in Heaven with Him with new bodies that are not given to sin.

HE TEACHES TRUTH

Another ministry of the Holy Spirit is to lead us into truth. Jesus said, "However, when He, the Spirit of truth, has come, He will guide you into all truth." (John 16:13) Sometimes as we are reading through the Bible things are hard to understand. Sometimes when you are listening to a Bible study, the pastor can be confusing or boring. The amazing thing to me is in each of those cases you can talk to the Holy Spirit through prayer and say to Him, "Lead me into all truth. What are you trying to say to me through this passage or through this message? Holy Spirit, speak to me through your word."

HE GIVES POWER

One final ministry of the Holy Spirit I want to touch on is that He has been given to us to empower us for life and ministry. In Ephesians 5, Paul shares with husbands how to love their wives. In the same chapter he shares with wives to respect their husbands, for children to honor their parents, and how employees and employers should interact with each other. Before Paul shares any of our responsibilities with each other, he tells us first to "be filled with the Holy Spirit." (Ephesians 5:18) Before you can be the husband God is calling you to be, or the wife, or the young person, or the employee, or employer, you must first be filled with the Holy Spirit.

Before we are going to be any good for God's Kingdom in whatever role and callings He has for us, we must be filled with the Holy Spirit. That is why Jesus told the disciples in Acts, not to try and do ministry on your own, you are to... "not depart from Jerusalem, but to wait for the Promise of the Father." (Acts 1:4)

Some of you are thinking, why? Why do I need to be filled with the Spirit to be who God wants me to be? I thought that at the moment of salvation I was baptized into the body of Christ by the Holy Spirit and He from that moment on was in my life to stay? If that is correct, and I believe it is by the way, then why do we need to be filled with the Holy Spirit?

THE HOLY SPIRIT'S RELATIONSHIPS WITH MAN

The reason comes from the understanding that Jesus spoke of there being three distinct relationships that the Holy Spirit would have with man. For each of them there is a Greek preposition in the scriptures. The first two come from John's gospel, "The Spirit of truth, whom the world cannot receive, because it neither sees Him, nor knows Him; but you know Him, for He dwells with you, and will be in you." (John 14:17, emphasis mine)

Jesus, teaching on the Holy Spirit, says He dwells with you, and will be in you. There we have the first two prepositions that show us the Holy Spirit's relationship with man today, after the cross. The first preposition is "with" or the Greek word "para". It means "alongside". This is true of every person throughout the world. The Holy Spirit is with them; alongside them. He is fulfilling His primary ministry to them-to convict the world of sin.

THE HOLY SPIRIT INDWELLS US

That is not true of the next relationship the Holy Spirit can have with man after the cross. The second preposition is "in" or the Greek word "en". You see, at the moment of salvation, the Holy Spirit takes up residence in our hearts.

In Acts 2:38, Peter tells the people to "repent" and "believe on the Lord." What happens as they do? They "shall be saved and receive the Holy Spirit." You see, at the moment we come to Christ, the Holy Spirit makes our heart His home-He is in us. That is why there seems to be more conviction after you receive Jesus as your Lord and savior. Before you were saved, you were convicted and knew you needed to get right with God, but the Holy Spirit was speaking to you from alongside. After conversion, He is speaking to you from your heart.

The Spirit is in you. Now having the Holy Spirit in you is a one-time thing. When Jesus said in John 14, "The Spirit will be in you," the word He chose to use is the one they would use for putting a dead body inside a coffin. Unlike being in a room, where you can come and go as you please, once you are in the grave, that shell of your body is going nowhere. When we receive the free gift of salvation Jesus offers us, the Holy Spirit takes up permanent residence in your heart. I don't believe that Christians today can pray the same prayer as King David in Psalm 51:11,

"Do not take your Holy Spirit from me." The Holy Spirit, by the grace of God is here to stay.

THE HOLY SPIRIT EMPOWERS AND DIRECTS US

However, there is one more preposition in the New Testament that deals with the Holy Spirit's relationship to man; it is found in Acts 1:8. "But you shall receive power when the Holy Spirit has come upon you; and you shall be witnesses to Me in Jerusalem, and in all Judea and Samaria, and to the end of the earth."

This third proposition is the word "upon" or in Greek "epi" and it has as its meaning the idea of overflowing within you, or shaping you, making you into another man or another woman. Sometimes we have the idea that being filled with the Spirit is a quantitative idea. When we are struggling with sin we may think we are a quart low on the Spirit of God.

We think of being filled with the Spirit like we are filled with food on Thanksgiving. I will never forget my first Thanksgiving as a married man. At that time all of our family lived close to my wife and me. This was great because my family liked to eat the Thanksgiving feast earlier, around two in the afternoon, and my wife's family liked to eat around five. I had a great plan to be disciplined and eat only a little bit at each meal, but once we got to my Mom's house, I smelled the home cooking. You can't disappoint mama, so I ate and ate until I was stuffed.

At five we headed over to my wife's parents and again I had a great plan to be disciplined, but you can't disappoint momma-in-law on your first Thanksgiving, so I stuffed myself once again. To make matters worse, my wife had said to me a couple of weeks previous to Thanksgiving, "I want us to have our own Thanksgiving meal. I want to make you a turkey." I responded to my wife by telling her, "Woman, do all that is in your heart!" After eating two complete meals, we went home about 7:30 and I ate my third Thanksgiving dinner in less than six hours. I was stuffed. I understood at that moment why gluttony is a sin!

We tend to think of being filled with the Holy Spirit the same way I approached Thanksgiving that year. I need more and more of the Spirit until I burst or stop sinning. That is a misunderstanding of what the Bible is trying to communicate. "Being filled" means to be controlled, or directed by.

We see that in Luke's gospel, when Jesus is teaching the Jewish leaders about who He is. He goes on to tell them, not only that He was the Messiah, but He is also going to be the Messiah of the Gentiles as well. If you know the New Testament, you know what happens next. The Jews can't handle it. It says they were "filled with wrath." (Luke 4:28) They were filled up- they were overflowing. It's the same idea.

That is interesting to me because once they were filled with wrath, they became different men. It changed who they were. They began to meet regularly and plan how they were going to kill Jesus. Now remember, these were the religious leaders: normally holy, God-fearing guys. Now, they are having murder meetings. We so often read our Bible with our lattes in our hand and a Danish and we think, "Well, isn't that nice, they wanted to kill Jesus." When we read passages like this, it isn't nice. Imagine if your pastor was meeting with others thinking about who he was going to kill. It might be time to change churches. This is what happened to them. They were filled with wrath, and it changed them.

This understanding of being filled tied into being shaped is why I believe Paul contrasts being filled with the Spirit with getting drunk in Ephesians. When you first encountered Ephesians 5:18, you may have thought Paul was trying to wrap up his message by throwing some different ideas together. "Don't be drunk, and… oh yeah, also be filled with the Spirit." These two ideas are not randomly put together.

Being drunk with wine and being filled with the Spirit are opposites in the moral spectrum; however, they both carry the same idea of controlling and shaping you. The word "dissipation" means "without limits" and it speaks of a person throwing away restrictions and living out of control, or in reality, being controlled by the substance. When you abuse drugs and alcohol you become something you are not.

On the other side of the coin, if you will be filled with the Spirit, God's Spirit will begin to control you, to shape you, to make you into something you are currently not. We need God's Spirit to become the men and women God wants us to be. We need to be filled with, and changed by God's Spirit.

PROOF OF THE FILLING-EVIDENCE OF A CHANGING LIFE

The book of Acts is a classic illustration of how this is so. The story of the Apostles in the gospels is not very flattering for them. I love the story in Luke 9, when the disciples went to the city of Samaria and the Samaritans rejected them. James and John then went to Jesus and said, "Lord, we know how to handle this rejection, let us call fire down from Heaven to consume them." (Luke 9:54) Don't you just see the Lord pulling His hair out, thinking to Himself, "You guys just don't get it." Jesus nicknames the two of them "The Sons of Thunder" because of their tempers. (Mark 3:17)

Once you understand that, consider John. The same guy

who wanted to call fire down from Heaven to kill people later wrote the epistle of First John. First John is a great little letter, and if you have ever read it, you know every page is about love. Love your brother, love your neighbor, and love the Lord. Every page says, "love, love, love." How does a "Son of Thunder" turn into the apostle of love? It was because he was filled with the Holy Spirit. He became another man.

What about Peter? The night before Jesus was crucified, Peter was approached by a little girl who asked him, "Aren't you with the Messiah?" (Matthew 26:69) Peter's response, "I never knew the man!" This same Peter, 50 days later, would stand up in front of not just a little girl, but thousands of people and declare to them, "This Jesus, whom you crucified is both Lord and Christ." (Acts 2:36) What change took place in him? What was the difference?

The difference was the Day of Pentecost. The Apostles already had the Holy Spirit living inside them before the Day of Pentecost. In John 20:22 Jesus said to the disciples, long before the Day of Pentecost, "Receive the Holy Spirit." Now, maybe I'm mistaken, but I believe if Jesus said to you, receive the Holy Spirit; guess what is going to happen? You are going to receive the Holy Spirit.

These guys already had the Holy Spirit in them, but on

the day of Pentecost, the Holy Spirit came upon them, filled them, and began to control them. For the apostles it wasn't a one-time thing; it was a daily submission that changed their lives.

I realize every day I am sinful and corrupt enough to ruin everything God has done in my life. That is why I begin each day, during my morning devotions by praying, "God, fill me with your Spirit. I want to be led by you. I want you to shape who I am. I am not naturally good; I am not naturally inclined to do the right thing. So Lord, empty me of myself and fill me with more of you."

I am not concerned with what title you want to give it. If you want to call what I am talking about being "filled with the Spirit", or "baptized by the Spirit", that's fine. If you want to call it the second, third, or fourth blessing, I don't care. I will leave that problem for others to argue over. I just know that I need less of me and more of Him; not just one time, but every single day.

Paul is literally saying to the Ephesian church, "Be being filled with the Spirit." Daily ask, daily seek for it by saying, "God, I need more of you, and less of me to become another man- different from the sinner that I am to the core."

A FINAL THOUGHT

Maybe you are thinking, "I do that, I ask the Lord to fill me. I ask Him almost every day. Why am I not experiencing the power of the Holy Spirit in my life if it is as simple as you say-to just ask?"

There is one last verse to consider. Paul, in 1 Thessalonians 5:19 says, "Do not quench the Spirit." The Holy Spirit in the Word is often compared to a fire. I believe that understanding this is the key to seeing how we can quench the Holy Spirit and His controlling, influencing effect in our lives.

A real fire can be quenched in two ways. You can add a foreign substance that is not part of the fire-producing process, such as water, dirt, or the chemicals from a fire extinguisher and the fire will go out. The other way you can quench a fire is to take away the fuel. If there is no fuel, a fire will not burn.

Quenching the Holy Spirit happens in the same way. If I am adding things to my life that the Lord says to avoid, those things will choke out the work of the Holy Spirit in my life. I can make all the excuses I want about how justifiable my sinful indulgences may be, and how I am saved by grace, but the truth remains-sin will quench the Holy Spirit in my life. If there is some sin that you are tolerating, repent right now and allow the Holy Spirit to burn bright.

Paul says in Romans, "For those who live according to the flesh set their minds on the things of the flesh, but those who live according to the Spirit, the things of the Spirit. So then, those who are the flesh cannot please God. But you are not in the flesh, but in the Spirit, if indeed the Spirit of God dwells in you. (Romans 8:5-9)

The word "dwells" there in verse nine does not mean the Holy Spirit is in you as the result of salvation. The word speaks of the Holy Spirit being at home in your heart. We all know what it is like to be at some hotel or friend's house when you just don't feel at home.

When I was growing up, my mom had a friend who had a son my age. I loved going over to his house because he had the complete set of Star Wars toys circa 1985. I would love to play in his room with him, but then he would ask if I wanted to spend the night. I couldn't stand spending the night at his house. It had nothing to do with him, but he had this pullout couch bed with a bar that would stick out of the middle of it, and even at seven years old, it ruined a good night's sleep. The other problem was his dog, who would jump up on the bed with you and begin licking you on the face. I loved that guy, but I was so uncomfortable at his house.

I wonder if the Holy Spirit feels that way sometimes with

us. He loves us because He is God, and God loves us, but we allow things in our hearts, and in our minds, and before our eyes that make Him respond, "I love you, but I am uncomfortable with this in your life." We need to let the Lord search our hearts and be willing to repent of those things that we are allowing into our lives that quench the power of the Holy Spirit.

The other way we can quench the Spirit is to not give Him the fuel He uses to set our life afire. Things like reading the Bible, a consistent prayer life, and attending a Bible teaching fellowship where the worship of God is prominent. These things don't earn God's favor or make Him bless us, but God certainly uses those things to give fuel to the Holy Spirit's work in our lives. As Paul said, when I set my mind on the things of the Spirit, I am going to walk in the power of the Holy Spirit. We have a choice to either live the Christian life that A.W. Tozer described without the Holy Spirit, "An impoverishment of Christian life and work." Or, we can live in and by the power of the Holy Spirit, the third part of the trinity in our lives.

FURTHER READING AND STUDY

- *"Basic Theology" by Charles Ryrie – available through Amazon*

- *"Systematic Theology" by Norman Geisler – available through Amazon*

- *"Living Water" by Pastor Chuck Smith – available through Amazon*

Man

His Creation, Fall & Salvation

"And the Lord God formed man of the dust of the ground, and breathed into his nostrils the breath of life; and man became a living being."

Genesis 2:7

There are many theories as to how man came into existence in the first place, but it all boils down to basically two points. Either man evolved through a series of naturalistic causes or man was created by someone or something supernatural. As I said in our first chapter, I believe there are good, rational and even intelligent reasons to believe man was created by God. The evidence for design in our bodies and in our universe, to me is just far too great to believe everything around us happened by chance.

Because I believe there are good reasons to believe in God and I believe there are also good reasons to believe in the validity of the Bible, I am going to approach the subject of man and his creation, fall and salvation from the perspective of believing what the Bible says.

IN THE BEGINNING

The Bible says that all human life began with our first parents, a couple named Adam and Eve. They were placed in the Garden of Eden and told by God to be fruitful, multiply, and fill the earth with their descendants. Because I believe the Bible to be a reliable source to learn about God and His creation, I take those facts on face value.

Have you ever thought about what man in his original creation was like? The Bible seems to paint a very different picture than our normal human experience today. I believe from Genesis 2:7 that man was created with two natures: a body and a spirit. We have a physical body that is made up of basically the same elements as dirt, which makes sense since Genesis 2 says God formed Adam out of the dust or dirt of the ground. I find it a real blow to my self-esteem to realize we as human beings are really just glorified dirt clods!

We have been given a physical body, and we are unique in God's creation. Genesis 2:7 says God, "Breathed into his nostrils the breath of life; and man became a living being." God created us with a body and with a spirit, that immaterial part of man that is eternal and connects with God.

It also seems from the early accounts in Genesis that man was originally created with his spirit foremost, as the directing force in his life. Adam's spirit was connecting with God as they walked together in the cool of the day (Genesis 2:16, 3:8). Adam's spirit was leading and directing his life, not his flesh. How wonderful it would have been to live in a time before sin dominated our thinking and lives. It would have been truly amazing, but all that changed with the events of Genesis 3.

THE BEGINNING OF THE END

God had given Adam and Eve all things freely to enjoy, with only one prohibition. They were not to eat of the fruit of the tree of the knowledge of good and evil that grew in the midst of the Garden of Eden. Some have wondered, "Why even put the tree there in the first place? Wouldn't it have been easier for all if there was no tree, and no forbidden fruit?" The answer is it may have been easier, but it would not have been as meaningful. You see, for love to be real, there has to be a choice.

When I asked my wife to marry me, there was no gun involved. She had a choice to marry me, or to reject my affection and move on in her life. The fact that she chooses to love me with all the other alternatives out there is one of the many things that makes my wife's love meaningful. To make the obedience of Adam and Eve meaningful there had to be a choice just as there is for every generations since. Are we going to choose to follow the Lord, His will, and His ways for our lives, or are we going to choose a different path?

Man's tempter came in the form of a serpent, possessed, or at least embodied, by the devil. As the serpent began to speak to Eve, his first temptation was to get Eve to doubt the Word of God. "Has God really said...?" was the question the enemy used to get Eve to doubt the Word of God. This is important for us to consider because the enemies' attack will always begin in the same way-trying to get us to question God's Word in our lives.

I find it very interesting how the attacks of Bible critics take on the same tone, "Has God really said?" There is an all-out effort to get you to doubt the Word of God, both academically and spiritually. "Do you really believe that sin is bad for you?" "Ok, I know that is what it says in that archaic book, the Bible." The enemy will whisper in your ear, "With all we understand in modern times, is that thing really wrong? Are you just a victim of Victorian-age morality?" The enemy will always get us to doubt the clear Word of God in our lives.

Eve, followed by Adam, did not resist temptation; they gave in to doubting God's word and disobeyed God's command by eating the forbidden fruit. Which, by the way, was not an apple! I read an article the other day by a so-called scholar who was mocking the Bible and claiming to have forever discredited the book of Genesis. His reason? He had discovered that apples do not grow naturally in the Middle East; therefore, the Genesis fall account had to be fictitious. There is one problem with his theory: the Bible never claims the forbidden fruit was an apple. Personally, I believe it was the avocado. Those things are delicious, but there is a lot of fat in those babies!

THE BEGINNING OF SIN

All kidding aside, when Adam and Eve partook of the fruit, something horrible happened-man's duel nature was reversed. Instead of the spirit being first and foremost, connecting with God, leading and directing man's life, now the body with its fleshly desires was first and foremost, and we have been fighting that battle ever since.

Not only was man's duel nature reversed, but man began to die both spiritually and physically. Adam and Eve knew right away something was wrong, but their first reaction was to try to hide from God. They tried to cover their sin with their own efforts by sewing fig leaves together and making their own clothes. Maybe that has been your reaction to the sin in your life. Maybe you have tried running from God. Maybe you have tried to do something yourself to make up for your sin, but no matter what we try, we can't remove our own guilt and shame.

Adam and Eve tried to cover their own nakedness by sowing together fig leaves, but God did something totally different. God killed an innocent animal to make a covering for their nakedness, and blood was shed to cover their sins. That idea of innocent blood covering sin would continue to dominate the Old Testament. God would eventually give His people, the Jews, an elaborate system of sacrifices for sin and rebellion, all requiring the death of an innocent animal. Normally it was a lamb without spot or blemish, which would be sacrificed to cover the sins of the people. The reason these Old Testament sacrifices were so important is they were all pointing to one future sacrifice, when Jesus, the spotless lamb of God would be killed for the sins of the world.

THE PERFECT SACRIFICE

Remember, we learned in chapter six that Jesus, who had always existed as part of the Trinity in eternity past, became flesh in Matthew 1, and Luke 2, to dwell among us. He did that to be a sympathetic high priest: to know what it was like to face what we face. He did it to show us what God was really like and communicate God's heart for mankind, but more than any other reason, Jesus became a man to die in our place.

You see, unlike us, Jesus lived a life completely without sin. He never dwelt on an impure thought. He never acted on an emotion of bitterness. He never stole anything. He never harmed anyone, yet He was treated on the cross of Calvary as if He was guilty of all of those things. Paul said, "For He made Him who knew no sin to be sin for us, that we might become the righteousness of God in Him." (2 Corinthians 5:21).

God, the Father, treated God, the Son, on the cross as

if He had lived my life and yours, with plenty to be ashamed of. God, the Father, treated God, the Son, as if He had lived my life and yours, so that God could treat you as if you had lived His. Salvation is the great exchange. His life for mine, my nature for His. It had to be this way. We are told that when Adam and Eve fell, it wasn't just them who were affected, but every one of their descendants, including you and me. Adam and Eve were created in innocence, but every human since them has had sin imputed and inherited.

INHERITED VERSUS IMPUTED

There is some discussion over whether sin is imputed or inherited. "Inherited" means you are born into it; "imputed" means it is given to you. If I inherit a million dollars, I have been born with this inheritance. If someone decides to give their wealth to me, it has been imputed. What has happened with sin? Do we get it from our parents, or is it imputed from someone else? The answer, I believe, is both.

SIN IS INHERITED

We are told this in Ephesians 2:3, "You were by nature children of wrath, just as the others." Psalm 51:5 tells us, "Behold, I was brought forth in iniquity and in sin my mother conceived me."

David is not saying that there is anything sinful about the conception process between a husband and his wife, nor is David saying he was conceived out of wedlock. What David is communicating is even at the very moment of conception, sin was in me-sin was there. I know the theory is that babies are innocent until we corrupt them, but if you truly believe that, in my opinion, you have not been a very observant parent.

I love my kids with all of my heart. My family is the most precious thing in this world to me, but I never had to teach them to sin. Just take away their toy, pacifier, bottle, or make them go to bed, and you will see what I am talking about. I am fully convinced that God made babies small because if they were full grown at times they would kill you! My little ones, as they were growing up would occasionally give me the look that said, "Give me back the pacifier if you know what's good for you, bub." We are born sinners.

Unfortunately our sin doesn't stop when we are infants. As we continue to grow, we continue to sin. "Sin" is a word that basically means, "to miss the mark". God's standard for you and me is perfection, but we have missed that mark both intentionally and unintentionally. I do things wrong I didn't even mean to do wrong. It is unintentional, but I still do it. Sadly we often sin intentionally, knowing full well what we are doing. The Biblical word for that type of sin is "transgression "and it means willful disobedience. It doesn't matter if you have sinned intentionally or unintentionally, you are still a sinner in need of a savior.

I have run into sweet grandmas who have told me, "I have never done anything intentionally wrong." Even thought I find that hard to believe, it still doesn't matter. Sin is missing the mark of perfection-the perfection of holiness God demands from our lives. We are all sinners in need of a savior because we are born with a sin nature. Sin is inherited, but it is also imputed.

SIN IS IMPUTED

"Therefore, just as through one man sin entered the world, and death through sin, and thus death spread to all men, because all sinned." (Romans 5:12) Not only do we get our sin nature from our parents at the moment of conception, but we also have sin imputed to us from Adam. He fell, and all of us are guilty as part of that. Now you may say, "That's not fair! Why do I get blamed for something someone else did?"

The answer to that is you would have done the same thing. Adam was our representative, and in a very real sense we were part of him. He lived in a perfect environment, had no dys-functional parents, received a perfect upbringing, yet Adam still chose to rebel. We would have done the same and we do the same every time we choose to ignore God's word and warnings and violate His commands.

Adam stood for us. He was our representative, and he failed, passing sin onto us. Before you get too upset, Romans 5 tells us we have another representative. Just as Adam stood for us and failed, so too Jesus stood in our place and had victory. Just as because of one man we are condemned, so too because of one man we are set free. Paul also said in the book of Romans, "Therefore, as through one man's offense judgment came to all men, resulting in condemnation, even so through one Man's righteous act the free gift came to all men, resulting in justification of life. For as by one man's disobedience many were made sinners, so also by one Man's obedience many will be made righteous." (Romans 5:18-19)

We are all guilty. We are all guilty because we have all sinned, but even beyond that, we are all guilty because all of us have had sin inherited and imputed to us from Adam and our parents. That is the bad news, but there is good news, too. The gospel, the good news is that through one man's obedience and sacrifice we can all be set free from the power and the penalty of sin. How does that happen?

BY FAITH

I have to believe what God says about me-that I am a sinner, separated from Him now and for all of eternity if something doesn't change. I need to come to Him by faith, and receive the free gift of salvation He purchased for me on the cross. Paul said, "If you confess with your mouth the Lord Jesus and believe in your heart that God has raised Him from the dead, you will be saved. For with the heart one believes unto righteousness, and with the mouth confession is made unto salvation." (Romans 10:9-10)

Some of you may be still lost in your transgressions. Some of you may still have the body, the flesh dominating your life. You need what Jesus did on the cross for you! You know you are a sinner. You know you are lost without Him, so it is time to turn to Him and be saved.

Now, can anyone be saved, or did God die for only a select few? Is your eternal destiny predetermined, or do you have a choice in the matter? We will examine those questions in detail in our next chapter together as we continue to look at man and how he is saved.

FURTHER READING AND STUDY

- "Basic Theology" by Charles Ryrie – available through Amazon

- "Systematic Theology" by Norman Geisler – available through Amazon

9

Man
His Salvation

"Oh, the depth of the riches both of the wisdom and knowledge of God! How unsearchable are His judgments and His ways past finding out!"

Romans 11:33

So far we have explored the fact that there are good reasons to believe God, something greater than you, exists. We have explored the reality that there are great reasons to believe the Bible to be a reliable source to learn about this God that is greater than us. In the Bible we discover that God is a trinity: God, the Father, God, the Son, and God, the Holy Spirit. We discover that as human beings we were lost in our transgressions and sins until God, the Son took on human flesh, became a man, and eventually died in our place. We have seen that Jesus has paid the penalty for our sin and offers us the free gift of eternal life, but the question still remains, can anyone receive that gift?

This question has caused great debate and argument in the body of Christ for almost 500 years. It is amazing how often in the church we argue over points of doctrine, and miss the point the Lord intends completely. We can argue over whether to use terms like baptized in the Spirit, versus filled with the Spirit, and miss the fact that God wants us to walk in the power of His Spirit, not in the power of our flesh. We can argue over whether or not the gifts of the Spirit are for today, or just a bygone era. We debate it so hotly we miss our greatest gift and commandment: to love one another. It has been my intention up to this point in this book to stay away from controversy on nuances of doctrine and simply lay a foundation for faith in your life.

HOWEVER...

With the debate in the church today over two subjects, Arminianism and Calvinism, I feel like the opinion I personally hold is sometimes seen as uneducated and unpolished, and I really take exception to that. Now don't misunderstand me, I do not feel like those who differ from me on opinions expressed in this chapter and in chapters 10-13 are themselves uneducated and non-thinkers, not in any way. I love and have great respect for friends of mine who are reformed pastors or Calvinists, and I have a great love and respect for those I know who hardly ever admit it, but are really of the Arminian persuasion. I know they understand what they believe and hold the opinions they do because they have thought through the matter themselves. I believe with all my heart God wants us all to spend far less time dividing over issues God will bring clarity on when we all stand before Him and more time loving one another and reaching a lost world that desperately needs Jesus and cares not for our petty disagreements. My heart is not to divide, but simply to explain a position.

A HISTORY LESSON

The history of the discussion really began when a reformed pastor ("reformed" meaning "non-Catholic", a pastor following the tradition of the reformation, but also "reformed" meaning "holding to the doctrines of reformed theology") by the name Jacobus Arminius began to question many of the conclusions of reformed theology. He left the pastorate of a reformed church in Amsterdam and became professor of theology at the University of Leyden. It was his series of lectures on election and predestination that led to a violent and tragic controversy.

After his death in 1609, his followers developed the Remonstrance of 1610, which outlined the "Five Points of Arminianism." This document was a protest against the doctrines of Reformed Theology, and was submitted to the state of Holland. The response by the followers of John Calvin, an earlier reformed pastor was the "Five Point of Calvinism". We'll discuss what those points are shortly.

I believe there are good reasons to hold a balanced, middle of the road view when it comes to the subject of God's sovereignty versus man's free will. For those who are joyfully unaware of the debate, the questions are these: are we saved because God chose us, elected us to be saved apart from anything we have ever or will ever do, or are we saved because we choose to respond to the conviction of the Holy Spirit in our lives? Are we saved because God sovereignly chose to do so in our lives, or are we saved because we responded to Him in our free will?

WHEN A TULIP IS NOT A TULIP

A brief description of what the acronym TULIP stands for will help set up this chapter and explain what is meant by the term "reformed theology". The "T" in TULIP stands for "Total Depravity". Reformed theology teaches that man is totally depraved to the extent that he cannot respond to God. The "U" in TULIP stands for "Unconditional election," meaning there are no conditions by which God elects man to be saved, including repentance.

The "L" in TULIP stands for "Limited Atonement" and it basically means Jesus' atonement on the cross was not for the whole world, but for only the elect. The "I" in TULIP stand for "Irresistible Grace" and that means God woos the elect with grace that cannot be resisted. Finally, the "P" in TULIP stands for "Perseverance of the Saints" and that basically means that all who are truly elected for salvation will persevere to the end.

Before we go any further, I totally understand that I gave you a very simplistic definition of TULIP. There is much more to reformed theology than an acronym. Many godly and wonderful men and women of faith in church history and today are what we term Calvinists. I read their books, I love them, and they are brothers and sisters in Christ in every way. I disagree with extreme Calvinism as you will see in just a moment, but I don't want to be misunderstood as attacking friends in the body of Christ. I just believe there are wonderful reasons to come down somewhere in the middle between two extremes.

A BALANCED APPROACH

It is my belief that the scripture teaches both sides. Not both sides of some man made "five points" exactly. I believe that God is sovereign, totally in control, and yet in His sovereignty He allows man to have a free will and holds him responsible for the decisions he makes with free will. I don't want to just state an opinion, but I want us to see it in the scriptures.

GOD IS SOVEREIGN

Man is not dictating to God what will happen. God is not sitting in heaven biting His nails hoping it all works out with mankind. We see from many scriptures in the Old and New Testament that God is totally in control. "The Lord of hosts has sworn, saying, 'Surely, as I have thought, so it shall come to pass, and as I have purposed, so it shall stand.'" (Isaiah 14:24). God does not bow to us. God says, "If I say it, it is going to happen." We also see this truth in the New Testament. "In Him also we have obtained an inheritance, being predestined according to the purpose of Him who works all things according to the counsel of His will." (Ephesians 1:11)

Paul is saying we have been chosen, not because of our purpose, but because of His. It wasn't because of the counsel of our will, but because He wanted it so. Now you might be thinking, "It sounds like you are a Calvinist. If God does what He wants and chooses us simply because of the counsel of His will, then how am I free? How do I have a free will?" Again, we must go to the scriptures!

MAN IS FREE

In both the Old and the New Testaments we see that we have a choice whether to follow the Lord or not. "Choose for yourselves this day whom you will serve, whether the gods which your fathers served that were on the other side of the River, or the gods of the Amorites, in whose land you dwell. But as for me and my house, we will serve the Lord." (Joshua 24:15) The New Testament says basically the same thing.

We all know what possibly the most famous verse in all of scripture says; "For God so loved the world that He gave His only begotten Son, that whoever believes in Him should not perish, but have everlasting life... He who believes in Him is not condemned; but he who does not believe is condemned already, because he has not believed in the name of the only begotten Son of God." (John 3:16, 18)

We are responsible to believe in the Lord, to respond to His wooing us in our lives and His convicting us of our sin (John 16:8). Whoever does can be saved, not just those whom God has chosen. You have a decision to make to serve the Lord. Jesus cried out to the people of Jerusalem, "O Jerusalem, Jerusalem, the one who kills the prophets and stones those who are sent to her! How often I wanted to gather your children together, as a hen gathers her chicks under her wings, but you were not willing!" (Matthew 23:37, emphasis mine)

God wanted to save them. God wanted them to be His, but the people of Jerusalem used their free will to reject Him and God honored their decision. You see, we find this balance that God is sovereign, yet man is free all through the scriptures. Consider John 1:12-13, "But as many as received Him, to them He gave the right to become children of God, to those who believe in His name: who were born, not of blood, nor of the will of the flesh, nor of the will of man, but of God." Do you see the balance?

Verse thirteen is often used to illustrate the belief that man has no free will. Many people point to this verse and say, "It's not the will of man." They neglect the part in verse twelve that says, "... to those who believed." Salvation comes to those who choose to believe and receive the Lord.

Some would argue, "Isn't God just inspiring people to do what He wants?" It seems like we have free will, but it is really just God working behind the scenes. That is what the great Bible teacher Jonathan Edwards believed was the answer to the problem, but hold on just a second. Do you believe God inspires people to sin against His will? Do you believe God inspired Judas to betray Christ? Do you believe that God inspired Eve to eat the forbidden fruit or the Jews to not believe in Jesus? Most of us would say, "Of course not." Again, we don't want opinions, we want the scriptures.

"Let no one say when he is tempted, 'I am tempted by God'; for God cannot be tempted by evil, nor does He Himself tempt anyone. But each one is tempted when he is drawn away by his own desires and enticed." (James 1:13-14) We are tempted by our own desires, our own free will, and our own nasty old sinful man. Truly Solomon, the wisest man who ever lived, summed it up pretty well when he said, "This I have found: That God made man upright, But they have sought out many schemes." (Ecclesiastes 7:29)

It may sound like I am one-sided in my opinion, but that is not true. If we go back to T-U-L-I-P and look at what the Bible says, again we find a balance.

TOTAL DEPRAVITY

Man is totally depraved to the extent that he cannot respond to God.

I believe the scripture teaches that we are, "Dead in our trespasses and sins." (Ephesians 2:1) I believe that "No one seeks after God." (Romans 3:11) Apart from Christ, we are dead; we don't seek after God, but what does that mean? The Calvinist will say, "A dead man can do nothing." and I agree. I can do nothing to save myself. I can do nothing to earn salvation and I will never deserve it. However, did Paul mean that we were dead in the sense that all of our capacity to respond to God is gone? I don't think so. Paul says, "For since the creation of the world His invisible attributes are clearly seen, being understood by the things that are made, even His eternal power and Godhead, so that they are without excuse, because, although they knew God, they did not glorify Him as God, nor were thankful, but became futile in their thoughts, and their foolish hearts were darkened."(Romans 1:20-21, emphasis mine)

God has revealed to the world, those who are dead in their trespass and sins, through the things in nature and things inside ourselves so no one will have an excuse not to respond to God. Think about it, Adam and Eve were dead in their sin, yet they could hear and respond to God as He was searching for them in the garden. It was not that they just could simply respond to the words, but if you read Genesis 3, you see they seem to understand what He was saying to them about the state of their souls. We cannot save ourselves. We cannot figure things out on our own. We need a savior! However, we can respond to God's invitation, and to Gods' wooing. We can, and we must!

UNCONDITIONAL ELECTION

There are no conditions by which God elects man to be saved, including repentance.

Are there conditions for salvation? Please understand, there are no conditions for God giving salvation. We do not earn salvation in any way. Salvation is completely His gift and His work. There are no conditions for God giving salvation, but there are conditions for receiving the salvation He purchased Himself. "Believe on the Lord Jesus Christ, and you will be saved." (Acts 16:31)

We are to believe. That term doesn't just mean to intellectually agree there is a God, but it means to cast all of who you are upon Him. We are to believe and we are to confess as Romans 10:9 says, "If you confess with your mouth the Lord Jesus and believe in your heart that God has raised Him from the dead, you will be saved."

Notice Paul uses the word "if"-if you confess. Are there conditions for the Lord to give salvation? No, you have not earned a thing. Are there conditions to receive salvation? Yes, you have to respond to what God initiates by believing and the outflow of believe, confessing and therefore responding to His initiation of salvation in your life.

LIMITED ATONEMENT

Jesus' atonement on the cross was not for the whole world, but for the elect.

Is Jesus' atonement limited? This is the one point of reformed theology that sometimes makes reformed pastors uncomfortable, but there is a Biblical balance here as well. Is Jesus' atonement limited? It is certainly "limited" in its application, for only those who believe and confess are saved. Without that understanding you would have "universalism" an unscriptural belief that the whole world will eventually be saved.

Jesus' atonement is limited in its application, but His atonement is not limited in its scope. "And He Himself is the propitiation for our sins, and not for ours only but also for the whole world." (I John 2:2) Jesus died for the sins of the whole world, not just a select few.

IRRESISTIBLE GRACE

God woos the elect with grace that cannot be resisted.

I agree, God's will is going to be accomplished, but can you as an individual resist what God wants to do including salvation? Of course you can. Remember Matthew 22:37? "O Jerusalem, Jerusalem, the one who kills the prophets and stones those who are sent to her! How often I wanted to gather your children together, as a hen gathers her chicks under her wings, but you were not willing!" God wanted to do something, and man resisted His will.

The reformed pastor might say, "We have free will after salvation, just not before. Everyone who He wants to be saved, will be saved. They are unable to resist His will." Well, what about 2 Peter 3:9? "The Lord is not slack concerning His promise, as some count slackness, but is longsuffering toward us, not willing that any should perish but that all should come to repentance." God is not willing that anyone should perish, and I Timothy tells us it is His desire that all men be saved. "... who desires all men to be saved and to come to the knowledge of the truth." (I Timothy 2:4)

If it is God's will and desire that all men be saved, but clearly all men are not saved. What that demonstrates is we have the ability to resist the will of God, not just in matters after salvation, but concerning the matter of salvation itself.

IS THERE AN ANSWER TO ALL OF THIS?

I believe it is rather foolish to think that a simple pastor has figured out what the church as a whole has been arguing about for hundreds of years, but I do think a proper understanding of I Peter 1:2 may shed some light on the subject for you as it has for me. Peter says that we are, "Elect according to the foreknowledge of God the Father."

Peter says we are "elect", chosen by God according to the foreknowledge of God. What is so amazing to me about this passage is it does not say we are elected "because" of the foreknowledge of God. Many pastors, including some of my Calvary Chapel friends, say things like, "He chose me because He knew I would choose Him." I really don't believe that is biblical. That would be election "because" of the foreknowledge of God, and that is not what the scripture says.

Of course, many reformed pastors will teach that we are elect "apart" from the foreknowledge of God. Nothing we will do or have ever done has affected God's decision to save us in any way. Peter does not say, "Elect apart from the foreknowledge of God."

Peter says we are "elect according to the foreknowledge of God." The phrase "according to" means in conjunction with, or working together with. You see, we are saved not because God knew what we would do, nor are we saved apart from that knowledge. Our salvation is based on what God wanted to do while working in conjunction with what He knew for sure we would do before we did it. Clear as mud, right?

Think of it this way: Something that boggles our little, puny human brains is that God is outside of time. He is not bound by the time constraints that we live in. God being outside of time is one of the reasons He can speak of the future as if it has already occurred, because to Him it has. In contrast to that, we live sequentially. We live in today, and one hour follows the next, and one event leads to another. God is outside of time, and so He sees it all happening at once. We live sequentially and we think sequentially. I asked my wife to marry me, and since I fooled her, she said yes! One event led to another. We live and think in sequence, but then we wrongly transfer that thinking to God.

"What happened?" we ask. "Did God choose me because I chose Him, or did I choose God because He chose me?" That is thinking in sequence, which God does not have to do. He is not sitting in Heaven waiting to see what you will do so He can respond. He has both known what you will do, and has chosen or elected you freely from before the foundation of the earth. Not because of what you would do, not apart from what you would do, but according, or in conjunction with what He knew for sure you would do.

THE MYSTERY OF GOD

Some people see the balance as a great contradiction. The great preacher, Charles Spurgeon, seemed to lean this way when he said, "God's sovereignty and man's free will are two parallel lines that only cross in the mind of God". This statement seems to make the whole matter a contradiction, but to me it's not a contradiction, it's a mystery. A contradiction would be me saying, "God is sovereign, but God is not sovereign." That is a contradiction. A contradiction is to say, "Man is free, but Man is not free." However, to say, "God is sovereign (completely in control) and yet man is free (totally free) is not a contradiction, but a mystery; a mystery we see all over the scriptures.

Personally, I think we need to take it back to where we started. "Oh, the depth of the riches both of the wisdom and knowledge of God! How unsearchable are His judgments and His ways past finding out! For who has known the mind of the Lord? Or who has become His counselor?" (Romans 11:33-34)

When did we figure out everything about God? It amazes me

on both sides of this debate that men think they have God and His ways totally figured out. His work of salvation totally fits in their little box of understanding. How does that bring God glory? Much of what we know and love about God is a mystery. Paul said in I Timothy 3:16, "Great is the mystery of godliness." Think about it with me. Do you totally understand the Trinity? Do you have that one figured out completely? God is three, but God is one? I know chapter four of this book was really good and helpful, but let's be honest, no you don't. You don't have it all down but you believe it because you see both in the scriptures. How about the incarnation? Do you have that one totally figured out? Jesus was fully God and at the same time fully man? How can you be 100 percent of two things? You can be 60/40, or 50/50, but 100 percent God and 100 percent man? It is a mystery. A mystery most of us accept because we see it in the scriptures. For some reason however, that doesn't seem to apply for some people to the mystery of salvation.

Don't run from the mystery! Some pastors, teachers, and Christians want to get rid of God's sovereignty and many more try to get rid of man's free will and responsibility, but to me both sides are important and I lose something when I pick one side or the other. You see, as I am going through the scriptures there are times when I am hit with a verse that lets me know God is completely in control and there are days I need to trust God like a

Calvinist, like God is in control (because He is) and no one in my life is going to rip off God's plan for me. I need that!

Then there are other times as I go through the Word and I read how God expects me to respond and obey, and I need that! I need at times to preach and live and believe like an Arminianist (which I don't think is a real word, but I am using it anyway), like God is going to hold me responsible for the decisions I make, because He will. Great is the mystery of godliness. Don't run from that; embrace that and let it lead you to worship someone that is far higher than you, one that you can trust with every fiber of your being. He has got you, and He is calling you to respond and obey.

FURTHER READING AND STUDY

- *"Chosen but Free" by Norman Geisler - available through Amazon*

- *"Calvinism, Arminianism & The Word of God" by Pastor Chuck Smith – free online*

10

Man
His Eternal Destiny

A DEFENSE OF THE DOCTRINES OF HEAVEN AND HELL

"And these will go away into everlasting punishment, but the righteous into eternal life."

Matthew 25:46

In our journey so far we have learned that there are good reasons to believe in a God, in something out there greater than you and me that created all we see around us. We have seen that the Bible is the most reliable source to learn about God, to learn about who He is and who we are in light of Him. We have seen the biblical balance between God's sovereignty and man's free will and this time we are going to explore more controversial waters, man's eternal destiny and the doctrines of heaven and hell.

For most of us we can't wait to get to heaven, but have you ever thought of what that experience is going to be like? Does the Bible give us any insight on the subject? On the other hand is the subject of hell. Is hell a real place? Will people actually spend eternity there? Why would a God who is loving create such a place like hell at all? These are all important questions we must address.

We begin with the most difficult subject first, the subject of hell. What does the Bible say about a future eternity separated from God? The first thing to consider is there are three main words that are used to describe hell in the Bible, and understanding them and their differences is very important

SHEOL: "THE ABODE OF THE DEAD"

One Hebrew word that is used often in the Bible to describe a destination for people after life on this planet is the word "Sheol." It is translated into English by using the words "grave", "pit", "hell" or even just transliterated, "sheol". In the Old Testament the word "sheol" is used to describe the dwelling place of both the righteous and the wicked after they departed this life. Now some say, "The righteous and the unrighteous going to the same place after death, that doesn't sound right!" Consider what the Word of God has to say.

We see "Sheol" used to describe the dwelling place of the righteous dead all throughout the Old Testament. Some examples are Psalm 16:10, 30:3, and Isaiah 38:10 which says, "I said, 'In the prime of my life, I shall go to the gates of Sheol; I am deprived of the remainder of my years.'" Isaiah, who definitely was righteous, talks about not wanting to die early, but also talks about where he is going to go, to Sheol.

We also see this word being used to describe the dwelling place of the unrighteous dead throughout the Old Testament. Some examples are Numbers 16:33, Job 24:19 and Psalm 9:17 which says, "The wicked shall be turned into hell, And all the nations that forget God." The word translated "hell" in Psalm 9:17 is "sheol", and it is speaking about the abode of the unrighteous dead.

Now why would both the righteous and the unrighteous

end up in the same place before the crucifixion of Jesus Christ? The answer is in the fact that through the Jewish sacrificial system, sin could be covered and forgiveness could be given, but sin could not be taken away. We are told this in Hebrews 10:4, "For it is not possible that the blood of bulls and goats could take away sins." The Jewish sacrifices made the people clean but it did not take away their sin. Therefore, when you died in the Old Testament, before the crucifixion of Jesus you could not enter straight into God's presence, for the blood of Jesus Christ had not yet taken away sin.

Where you ended up, good or bad, was Sheol, the abode of the dead. Some of you are thinking, "Well that doesn't sound very fair or right, I thought the righteous and unrighteous were always separated in death?" To that I would say, "you are right, they were." Now how is that possible? We see the answer to this in our next word that describes "hell" in the Bible and that is the Greek word "Hades."

HADES: "THE ABODE OF THE DEAD"

The Greek word "Hades" can be translated into English using the words "grave", "pit", "hell" or even just transliterated, "Hades". Maybe you can see that "Hades" is the Greek equivalent of the Hebrew word "Sheol". In other words they are two names in two different languages for the same place, the abode of the dead before the death and resurrection of Jesus Christ.

As I said a moment ago, even though there was one place everyone would go after death before the cross, the unrighteous dead and the righteous were still separated in Hades or Sheol. We see this in a story Jesus told in Luke 16. First of all, this is not a parable as some of your Bibles might say in the title. Those titles in your Bible are not are not inspired. Parables are fictional stories that help illustrate a point and they are full of the phrases such as "Like or as". For instance, "The Kingdom of God is like a mustard seed," (Luke 13:18-19.)

The story in Luke 16 is not a parable; Jesus is teaching what would happen after death, again before the crucifixion. Jesus says the rich man and Lazarus are both in Sheol or Hades, the abode of the dead, but there seems to be two sides, or two compartments. One is called, "Abraham's bosom" (Luke 16:22), and Jesus also calls it "Paradise" in Luke 23:43. These are terms used by Jesus and Jewish scholars to describe where the righteous believers would go after death. Now the unrighteous dead would also go Hades or Sheol, but they would end up in another part or compartment, described by Jesus as "a place of torment." (Luke 16:23)

This section of Hades or Sheol is still not eternal hell as

we think of it, but a horrible holding place for the unrighteous dead until they are resurrected to stand before the Great White Throne Judgment at a later time. I believe this section of Hades or Sheol is where unrighteous dead have gone and still go after they take their last breath in this life.

Revelation describes what will happen to that compartment of Hades or Sheol and the people located there at the time of the Great White Throne Judgment. "And I saw the dead, small and great, standing before God, and books were opened. And another book was opened, which is the Book of Life. And the dead were judged according to their works, by the things, which were written in the books. The sea gave up the dead who were in it, and Death and Hades delivered up the dead who were in them. And they were judged, each one according to his works. Then Death and Hades were cast into the lake of fire. This is the second death. And anyone not found written in the Book of Life was cast into the lake of fire." (Revelation 20:12-15)

YEEVVA OR GEHENNA: "HELL"

After the Great White Throne Judgment, Hades is emptied into the Lake of Fire, and it is here the unrighteous will spend eternity. It is this place that we are thinking of when we think of eternal hell. Jesus used the Greek word "yeevva" or as it is transliterated into English more commonly "gehenna" or "hell" to describe this place.

In the New Testament hell is described as...

- A place where their worm does not die and the fire is not quench–Mark 9:46

- A place of outer darkness–Matthew 8:12

- A place of Weeping–Matthew 25:30

- A place of Gnashing of teeth–Matthew 25:30

- A place of Wailing–Matthew 13:42

- A place of Flames–Luke 16:24

- A place of Everlasting punishment–Matthew 25:46

- A place of Eternal destruction, a place where you are cast away from the presence of the Lord–2 Thessalonians 1:9

All but one of these passage are descriptions Jesus gave of hell. I mention that to you because sometimes we think Jesus never even talked about hell, or I have heard it said that Jesus was too loving to talk about hell. The truth is, Jesus, who was the most loving man to ever walk the planet mentions hell over 70 times in His teachings. Jesus talked more about hell than about heaven because as someone who loves you, He doesn't want you to end up there.

IS THERE AN ALTERNATIVE TO HELL?

To me the Bible is very clear and straightforward concerning hell, but the Devil, who remember, is a liar (John 8:44) has developed some more acceptable ideas for man to consider. Some prevailing ideas today are:

- **Annihilation:** the belief that the unrighteous simply cease to exist.

- **Reincarnation:** the belief we move on to another life form.

- **Universalism:** the belief that eventually everyone goes to heaven.

Now please don't misunderstand me. I wish those alternatives were true. Well, I really don't want to come back as a worm, but you know what I mean. I wish hell was not real, or at least not forever, but I believe the Bible paints a different picture.

Annihilation, as much as I personally in my finite understanding would prefer it to be true, especially compared to the truth of eternal hell, is flawed because of a few things that are said in Revelation chapter 19 and 20.

Revelation 19:20 says, "Then the beast was captured,

and with him the false prophet who worked signs in his presence, by which he deceived those who received the mark of the beast and those who worshiped his image. These two were cast alive into the lake of fire burning with brimstone." (Emphasis mine) Now, this "lake of fire" is the same lake of fire that everyone whose name is not written in the book of life will end up in according to Revelation 20:12-15. Consider what we just read in Revelation 19:20 with what is said in Revelation 20:10

"The devil, who deceived them, was cast into the lake of fire and brimstone where the beast and the false prophet are. And they will be tormented day and night forever and ever." Revelation 20 takes place at least 1,000 years after Revelation 19 and notice hell is not where the beast and the false prophet used to be before they were annihilated, but where they still are and where they will be forever and ever.

Reincarnation, which obviously is not believed by most Christians, is also biblically flawed because of what is said in Hebrews, "it is appointed for men to die once, but after this the judgment," (Hebrews 9:27) We do not live over and over again in successive lives, trying to get things right, but we live once and then we will stand before the Lord.

Finally, universalism is flawed, again as much as I personally love the idea of everybody will eventually go to heaven, because of something Jesus Himself said in Matthew 25:46, "And these will go away into everlasting punishment, but the righteous into eternal life." We don't all end up in the same place. As I said before the idea of eternal hell does bring up some important objections we must address. In our next chapter, I would like to tackle three of them.

FURTHER READING AND STUDY

- *"Basic Theology" by Charles Ryrie – available through Amazon*

- *"Systematic Theology" by Norman Geisler – available through Amazon*

- *"Answers to the tough questions on Hell" DVD by Charlie Campbell – available on Alwaysbeready.com*

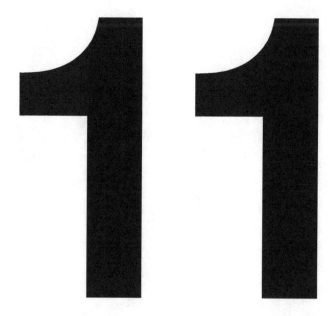

Man

His Eternal Destiny (Part Two)

ARE THERE ANY VALID OBJECTIONS TO HELL?

"And these will go away into everlasting punishment, but the righteous into eternal life."

Matthew 25:46

The subject of the existence of hell and it's consequences raise a lot of objections, even among Christians. In this chapter, I want to look at the three most common protests and how they line up with what we see in God's Word.

A GOD OF LOVE WOULD NEVER SEND SOMEONE TO HELL.

The thing we must consider when answering this objection is, "Where did we get the idea that God is loving? Buddhists don't believe God is loving. The Quran says Allah loves everyone except sinners. (Quran 2:190) The Hindus don't teach God is loving. So where do we get this idea? We got this idea that God is loving from the Bible. "God is love." (I John 4:16.)

It is the Bible, and only the Bible that teaches God is love. The problem with that is it is also the Bible that teaches us about eternal hell. (Matthew 25:46) People like to treat the Bible like it is a salad bar. "Oh I like that, God is love, I like that, oh, I don't like that, eternal hell, that doesn't make any sense." It's not a salad bar, eternal hell isn't a tomato, it's the Word of God and we must take all of it, the stuff we love and understand and are for, and those doctrines that are hard for us to grasp and reconcile.

It is true God is loving, but God is also righteous and just and will deal seriously with sin. God in His love has made a way to forgive sinners. People don't have to go to hell, they have a choice. He doesn't want to send you to hell, but you can choose to deny Him. He will not stand in your way if that is where you want to go, if you refuse to acknowledge Him as Lord in this life.

GOD WON'T SEND GOOD PEOPLE TO HELL.

Some people realize they deserve hell, but they consider Grandma Betty and cousin Earl and they begin to object, "It makes no sense for God to send good people to hell simply for not believing in Jesus." We know we deserve judgment, but what about all those good people? Now, on this one I agree with you. God will not send good people to hell, but here is the problem, there are no good people. This is true according to the Bible:

- Luke 18:19–no one is good but God.

- Romans 3:10–there is none righteous, no, not one.

- Isaiah 53:6–all we like sheep have gone astray.

This is true according to the Bible but it is also true according to life. You see you know deep down you deserve judgment but you think Grandma Betty is good and does not. However the reason you feel that way is you don't really know Grandma. Grandma, if she is honest, would be the first to tell you she is a sinner deserving of judgment, and if she is not honest and won't admit that, then well it just proves my point! We are all sinners. The good news in that is God has provided a way for sinners to be saved, for unrighteous folks like you and me to put on His righteousness. It's the gospel!

- We are all sinners–Romans 3:23

- The wages for that sin is death–Romans 6:23

- But the gift of God is eternal life through Jesus Christ –Romans 6:23

- For Christ died for us, took our place–Romans 5:8

And you can receive forgiveness, "By believing in your heart, and then confessing with your mouth" (Romans 10:9)

The other part of that objection is that God would send someone to hell simply for not believing in Jesus. We need to understand why salvation really does come down to what you do with Jesus. The gospel of John says, "And when He has come, He will convict the world of sin, and of righteousness, and of judgment: of sin, because they do not believe in Me;"(John 16:8-9)

John was saying when the Holy Spirit comes He is going to convict the world of sin. Why? What sin? The sin of not believing in Jesus. Not believing that He is your savior, your answer to salvation. Think it through with me.

You have a world of sinful men and women and as we have already discovered, not one of them is truly righteous. So the plan to deal with this is your son, your only son, is going to go to them. He's going to become a man, live a sinless life, never doing anything wrong, and then He is going to be brutalized by these unrighteous people, taking their place on a cross. You go with this as a Father not because you want to see your son harmed, but because you understand He is the only one who can stand in their place, for He is the only one who is truly righteous. You go along with this plan, your son is sacrificed and then the same people He died for say, "Why is that the only way? Why do I have to believe in Jesus?"

The answer is because there is no other way! You didn't live sinless, you didn't even live up to your own standard of righteousness. "My son died as the only option to save mankind and now you want to know why He is the only way?" If it were my son and he said, "Dad I will die for those people." If I let it happen because there was no other way, and then those people he died for said, 'I don't know if I like that." do you know what I would do? If I were God they wouldn't be allowed to take another breath, but God is gracious to give us a lifetime to see the truth. However, if we want to live a life without Him? If we want to be judged on our own works? If we refuse the free gift that He has paid for with His own blood? Then God is more than justified to say, 'there is no other way' and give us what we want. That leads to the third and final objection.

WHY ETERNAL HELL?

I once had a young student ask me a question that I took a while to answer because I had to really think it through. This student said to me, "I understand why those who will not receive Jesus' free gift of salvation can't go to heaven, but why hell? Why would God create a place that is so awful instead of just once and for all judging those who do not want to walk with God?"

It is a great question. I personally believe the answer is twofold. The first part of the answer comes from the fact that man is eternal. God created us in His likeness and of course He is eternal. So though our bodies are temporary, the real you is going to live forever and that is either part of the wonder or part of the problem. We think, "Why doesn't God just annihilate the people who reject Him?" Could it be that it is simply not that simple? God created us eternal and eternality does not just go away?

The other answer in my opinion is God did not create hell so awful because He is mean and vengeful and He wanted hell to be this awful place. But because He was going to create a place where He was not; and anywhere He is not is just that bad. Does that make sense? When we think of evil and why God allows evil to exist, it is not that God created evil. Evil is the absence of doing things God's way. God commands us not to kill, people disobey and the result is evil. Could it be that we don't truly understand how wonderful it is to live in a world where God is omnipresent, and that part of what makes heaven be heaven is the fact that we are in His presence? What if what makes Hell so awful is that it is a place where God has chosen not to be? A place where people who don't want God truly finally get what they want, but only too late do they discover the horror of what they are actually wanting?

I don't know if this truly answer the question and I'm sure smarter men than me can blow holes in the argument, but I have a hard time explaining away something Jesus talked so frequently about. At the same time I am well aware of the nature of God and how wonderfully loving He is. For me these answers help, hopefully they do for you as well.

WHERE ARE THE RIGHTOUS DEAD NOW?

Now before we close this chapter, a quick word on the much better alternative, heaven! Last chapter I shared the fact I believe in Old Testament times everyone, good or evil ended up in Sheol or Hades. The righteous dead went to a different part than the unrighteous dead. The righteous were not suffering like the rich man, not destined for Gehenna, like the unrighteous dead, but instead in that compartment of Hades made for the righteous called "Abraham's bosom" and "Paradise" by Jesus.

I believe the other compartment of Hades made for the righteous no longer exists, for when Jesus died on the cross sin was no longer just covered, it was taken away. Jesus, it seems in those three days between His death and resurrection, took the righteous dead in Hades, in Sheol, and took them to the presence of God, to what we would think of as heaven.

You see, after the resurrection of Christ, the location of "paradise" was changed from a compartment of Hades or Sheol to the presence of God. We see this when the apostle Paul says that he was "caught up to the third heaven... into Paradise" (2 Corinthians 12:1-4) "Paradise", therefore, now is associated with the immediate presence of God.

What did Paul mean when he said he was "caught up the third heavens?" Well, just like there are three words that the Bible translates as hell, there are three ways the Bible uses the term "heaven":

- Where the birds fly-"Who teaches us more than the beasts of the earth, And makes us wiser than the birds of heaven?" Job 35:11

- Where the Sun and Stars are-"In them He has set a tabernacle for the sun, Which is like a bridegroom coming out of his chamber, And rejoices like a strong man to run its race. Its rising is from one end of heaven, And its circuit to the other end;" Psalm 19:4-6

- Where the Lord's Throne is-"The LORD is in His holy temple, The LORD's throne is in heaven;" Psalm 11:4

Heaven, as we now think of it, is today being in the presence of the Lord as Paul also said in 2 Corinthians 5, "We are confident, yes, well pleased rather to be absent from the body and to be present with the Lord."

For the righteous who die today, and ever since the cross, there is not some holding place. That kind of concept is a church tradition, and not from the Bible. No, the Bible makes it clear that your last breath on earth will be followed by your first breath in heaven, in the presence of God. Now, what is that going to be like? What can we expect in heaven?

HEAVEN: A PREVIEW

So often I think the world thinks of heaven as a never ending church service and that doesn't sound too great, even to me as a pastor. Some think of heaven as sitting on a cloud playing a harp with some fat baby angel. Again no one including myself is very interested in that for eternity. Those ideas, however, I find completely wrong biblically.

The fact is we are not told much about what heaven will be like. One of the reasons I believe that is so is because if we truly knew what amazing things await us, many might be tempted to start the process a little early. When Paul the apostle got a little glimpse into heaven he described it this way... "inexpressible words, which it is not lawful for a man to utter." (2 Corinthians 12:4)

This is amazing to me because Paul was the man who could say anything five different ways and in five different languages. Paul, the master of words, found no words to describe the wonders of heaven. I wonder if we are not told too many details because the temptation would be too great to just end it here and get on with eternity there. Even though we are not told much, what we do know is still mind blowing. Consider a couple of things.

IN HEAVEN THERE WILL BE NO MORE PAIN, SIN, OR SUFFERING

As wonderful as this life can be it also can be really sad and disappointing with all the pain and sickness and death. In heaven all of that is removed. Who knows what life is really supposed to be like? Some Christians who are scientists have speculated that in the Garden of Eden the air was far more oxygenated that it is now. That would mean for Adam and Eve it was even fun to breathe and you could run and not get tired. Who knows how much the curse of sin has really brought to this world and our standard of living and what it will be like to live in a world the way God intended it to be.

IN HEAVEN THINGS WILL BE MADE RIGHT

Many times Jesus said that in heaven "the last will be first and the first will be last." (Matthew 19:30) Do you go through life and sometimes think things aren't fair? Why is that guy blessed, and that one over there seems to get all the bum luck? He loves the Lord and yet has to experience trial after trial. It doesn't make sense, until you factor in heaven.

Heaven is the great equalizer where God is going to set things right, the way they should be. You take ministries for example. My God-given ministry is to teach the Word of God to people and if I can be honest, that is not a real difficult ministry. Oh, I am not saying it's not important or I don't work hard at it and there are certainly difficult moments in it, but when all things are consider I am pretty blessed to do what I do.

Let's be honest, I have received a lot of my reward right here and now in this life, as people come and tell me how blessed they were with a study or the books. I sometimes don't know if there will be reward left when I step into eternity. Some of you faithfully pray, some of you faithfully give, and some of you faithful serve your unbelieving husband or wife. No one notices, no one thanks you for your ministry and sometimes the devil whisper in your ear that nobody cares and this is not fair. In those times we must remember heaven. Great is your reward in heaven! Heaven, where the curse is reversed and life is as God intended, where things are made right, where the last are finally first.

HEAVEN IS A PLACE WHERE THERE IS FULLNESS OF JOY

King David said in Psalm 16:11, "in your presence is fullness of joy and at your right hand are pleasures forever more." This is so often not how we think of it. We get tricked by our enemy into thinking that serving the world and our flesh is awesome fun, but then you die and go to hell and who wants that? So we will serve the Lord, which is hard and boring and then we get to go to heaven, so let's drudge on. No way! "In His presence is fullness of joy."

The reality is friends, we go through this life, and I believe God gives us glimpses of heaven. You hold your newborn child, you see a sunset, you achieve something in business, you fall in love, this is not the order of course, but in all these experiences something inside you fills with joy.

However, then that child spits up on you, the sunset fades, the next deal doesn't work out and your dream man disappoints and you wonder why. Why I am not fulfilled, why am I not happy? The answer is because God has created you for another place, and it seems like we are the first generation not to understand that. We are looking for happiness here in this life only. We do everything we can to amass things here. We try everything we can to extend this life any way we can and we grieve when a young man and women dies, saying "what a tragedy they died so young, they missed out on so much life."

We miss the reality of heaven, that what we are looking for here, fullness of joy, will only be found there in His presence. Heaven will not be sitting on a cloud playing a harp or an endless church service; it will be the fulfillment of everything you have been longing for in the core of your soul. Let heaven be more than a someday destination but a motivation for the rest of your life.

What will your eternal state be? Heaven or Hell? It is my job to tell you the truth; it is your job to make a decision. Some of you are headed toward heaven; some of you have put yourself under the wrath of God. He is just, He will judge sin, but because He is loving and merciful, and gracious, He sent Jesus to bear that wrath, to bear your sin. If you refuse Jesus, you will be justly dealt with in the wrath of God and you will have no one to blame but yourself. I know that message is not popular today, but it is the truth, and I love and fear God too much to not tell you the truth. What you do with truth is up to you.

FURTHER READING AND STUDY

- *"Basic Theology" by Charles Ryrie – available through Amazon*

- *"Systematic Theology" by Norman Geisler – available through Amazon*

- *"Answers to the tough questions on Hell" DVD by Charlie Campbe – avaiable on Alwaysbeready.com*

12

Man
His Future

AN EXPLANATION AND DEFENSE OF THE RAPTURE
OF THE CHURCH

"Then we who are alive and remain shall be caught up together with them in the clouds to meet the Lord in the air. And thus we shall always be with the Lord. Therefore comfort one another with these words.."

I Thessalonians 4:17-18

As we now come toward the end of the book we are going to shift gears from things we can be very certain about to the subject of prophecy. I believe we can be certain whether or not there is a God, whether or not the Bible is trustworthy to learn about that God. I believe we can be certain about the Trinity, the deity of Jesus, the importance of the Holy Spirit or the need for salvation for all of mankind. When it comes to the subject of prophecy, we now enter into the realm of opinion.

When dealing with matters of prophecy I often think of what it must have been like to be an Old Testament scholar in the years before Jesus was born, discussing your opinion about the coming of Messiah. Some would have said with absolute certainty, "We know that Messiah will be born in Bethlehem for it says in Micah 5:2, 'But you Bethlehem Ephrathah, though you are little among the thousands of Judah, yet out of you shall come forth to Me, the One to be the ruler in Israel.'" Others would then pipe up and say, "That's crazy, it's clear from Hosea 11:1 that Messiah will come out of Egypt for Hosea says, 'Out of Egypt I called My son.'"

Then you would have had those from 1st United Nazareth Fellowship that would have said, "You Bethlehemites and Egyptites are both heretics, don't you read your Bible? It is clear that Messiah will be from Nazareth for the prophets say the Messiah shall be called a Nazarene. (Matthew 2:23) I just picture them dividing, having their various conferences and making fun of the others who believe different things.

When Jesus actually did show up, we know in hindsight that He was born in Bethlehem. As an infant His family fled to Egypt and then as a young man His family moved back to Israel and Jesus eventually grew up in Nazareth. So if you are following what I am saying, all three things the Old Testament scholars would have argued about ended up being true, albeit in a much different way then most of those Old Testament scholars probably expected. To make matters worse of course, those Old Testament scholars then missed Jesus completely as they held desperately to their preformed opinions of the way Messiah was surely going to be and behave. I remind you of that, as we step into the subject of prophecy. The reality is what we should know for certain is this; that the Bible is true, and on the subject of prophecy, we simply have opinions. The Bible will be right in the end, we just think we are. It is wonderful to have strongly held opinions, we just need to remember that is exactly what they are and actually love one another while holding those opinions.

ESSENTIALS VERSUS NON-ESSENTIALS

I love what Rupertus Meldenius once said, "In essentials

Unity, in non-essentials Liberty, in all things Charity." I bring this up because the first few chapters of this book I really believe are essentials. God is real, and the Bible is a reliable source to learn about God, who is a Trinity consisting of God the Father, God the Son and God the Holy Spirit. We are saved by grace through faith in the work of Jesus Christ on cross for you and for me. Those are essentials. Prophecy is a non-essential. No one will miss out on heaven because they believed or didn't believe in the rapture of the church, the tribulation period or the millennial reign of Christ. These are non-essentials.

We need, however, liberty and charity with these things, room to understand why we believe the things we do and no matter what, love toward one another. I am well aware there are those who come down on my side of the opinion fence that can be dismissive and cold toward those who don't believe in a literal rapture, tribulation or millennium. But it seems to me lately if you hold to a pre-tribulation view of the rapture, you are seen by many as an uneducated hick who has never really thought these things through. This is simply not true. I believe what I do not because I am a Calvary Chapel Pastor or because Pastor Chuck believed these things, but because as I have studied the Word for myself, I believe these things to be the truth. It is my purpose in this chapter to present a good explanation of what the rapture of the church is, why I believe the rapture will happen before the tribulation period and why I believe it is an important belief not to be dismissed off hand. I love and respect those who have different beliefs in non-essentials and I believe there is reason for the feeling to be mutual.

WHAT IS THE RAPTURE?

We need to start out by defining what the rapture is, for some may have no idea what I am talking about. The rapture of the church is a yet future event where Jesus comes and takes those who are believers to heaven without them having to experience death. The teaching comes from three main passages in the New Testament. Paul begins to explain the rapture in I Corinthians, "Behold, I tell you a mystery: We shall not all sleep, but we shall all be changed, in a moment, in the twinkling of an eye, at the last trumpet. For the trumpet will sound, and the dead will be raised incorruptible, and we shall be changed. For this corruptible must put on incorruption, and this mortal must put on immortality." (I Corinthians 15:51-53)

Paul wants to share with us a mystery. Now, a mystery in the Bible is not like we think of today. A mystery in today's understanding is something really hard to figure out. A mystery in the biblical sense means something that was previous concealed that is now going to be revealed. In the Old Testament there were only hints at the doctrine of the rapture, verses like Isaiah 26:20, "Come away my people, enter your chambers, and shut your doors behind you, hide yourself, as it were for a little moment until the indignation is past."

The rapture of the church, Jesus hiding away the church during the Great Tribulation is something I think is hinted at in the Old Testament, but Paul is telling the Corinthian church it is time to unveil this truth completely. "Not all will sleep," Paul says in verse 51. This does not mean that some of us have trouble getting our 40 winks in every night; "sleep" is a biblical word for death, the death of believers. When believers die we do not cease to exist, but start to really experience life in the presence of the Lord. Paul the apostle comes up with a different word to describe the life ending event for a believer here on planet earth.

He says we will not all die, but we all must be changed. We are not going to spend eternity in these sinful, frail bodies, and to that I say, "Praise the Lord"! I get up sometimes in the morning and my body aches and cracks, I don't want to live that way forever. We need new bodies, without sickness, death or sin, by the way.

This transformation from our shell that we live in currently into new bodies, Paul says, will happen "in a twinkling of an eye." That means in less time than it takes to blink, God will change a group of Christians who will still be alive when Jesus comes for His church and give them new bodies suitable for the heavenly environment.

DETAILS OF THE RAPTURE

Paul also says that the timing for this event will happen at the last trump, which we will explain in just a minute, but first Paul gives us more needed information. In I Thessalonians 4:15-18 he says, "For this we say to you by the word of the Lord, that we who are alive and remain until the coming of the Lord will by no means precede those who are asleep. For the Lord Himself will descend from heaven with a shout, with the voice of an archangel, and with the trumpet of God. And the dead in Christ will rise first. Then we who are alive and remain shall be caught up together with them in the clouds to meet the Lord in the air. And thus we shall always be with the Lord. Therefore comfort one another with these words"

Again, Paul says there is coming a time when Jesus is going to take His church from the earth, I believe, to avoid the Great Tribulation period. There will be Christians who have died, obviously, at that point in history and there will also be Christians who will still be alive at that time. Those who are dead will be res- urrected to be with the Lord and those who are alive and remain on earth will be 'caught up' with them in the clouds, to meet the Lord in the air.

Here's the context for what Paul is saying. He was dealing with new believers in Thessalonica who had friends who were believers and had died. There began to be a false teaching that those who had died had missed the coming of Jesus for His church. Paul clarifies and lets this church know that is not true. If you have died when it is time for Jesus to get His church, He will resurrect you, if you are alive when Jesus comes for His church you will be "caught up."

IS THE RAPTURE IN THE BIBLE?

Some people do not accept the rapture because they say the word, "rapture" never appears in the Bible. They are correct if you have an English Bible. The Greek word translated "caught up" is "harpazo" in Greek, but if you have a Latin Bible the word is "rapturous" which is where we get the English word "rapture." Personally I don't care if you want to call it the "rapture", the "catch up" or the "Harpzo", I just believe there is coming a time when not all believers will die. They will need to get new bodies in order to be with Him, so God will catch them up into heaven and change them in a moment of time.

Paul introduces the subject in I Corinthians, he further explains the rapture in I Thessalonians, which leads some to believe that this rapture is just a Pauline doctrine, (a doctrine taught by Paul) but I believe the subject was actually first taught by Jesus in John 14:1-3. "Let not your heart be troubled; you believe in God, believe also in Me. In My Father's house are many mansions; if it were not so, I would have told you. I go to prepare a place for you. And if I go and prepare a place for you, I will come again and receive you to Myself; that where I am, there you may be also." (Emphasis mine)

Jesus is comforting His disciples that even though He is going away, He is going to prepare a place for them. Then Jesus says, and if I go, (which He did) I will come again and receive you to Myself. Jesus says I will come again and take you to heaven. You see, I think some think that the rapture is some new weird doctrine, but in reality "rapture" is just how God gets alive people to heaven and He has been doing it since the book of Genesis. Consider these "raptures" in the Bible:

Enoch was not for God took Him. Genesis 5:24

Elijah was "caught up" into heaven in a whirlwind. 2 Kings 2

Paul was "caught up" into the third heaven. 2 Corinthians 12

Two Witnesses are told to "come up here" to heaven. Revelation 11

Jesus, after His resurrection was "carried up" into heaven. Luke 24

The Rapture is not some weird new thing God is doing, it is how He gets alive people to heaven. The rapture as we think of it isn't new, it's just the first time God has tried group travel!

IS THE RAPTURE A NEW TEACHING IN THE CHURCH?

Another problem some people have with the rapture is they say, "Well the rapture may not be a new thing for God but the idea of God rapturing the church really is a new teaching. The first man to teach the rapture was a man by the name of John Darby who came up with this teaching in 1820 after hearing it from an epileptic girl he was friends with."

I have found that not to be historically accurate. First of all I believe Jesus and Paul the apostle first taught that Jesus was going to come back to earth and take Christians to heaven. Also, consider this quote by Ephraim the Syrian from 373 AD.

"For all the saints and elect of God are gathered prior to the tribulation that is to come and taken up to be with the Lord lest they see the confusion that is to be overwhelming in the world because of sin. Most dearly beloved believe the Holy Spirit who speaks in us–now we have spoken before because the end of the world is near, we ought to understand brothers what is im-minent—that is, all saints and the elect of the Lord will be gathered together in the clouds before the tribulation which is about to come and are taken to the Lord in the sky in order that they may not see at any time the confusion in the world which overwhelms this world because of sin."[1]

In fact, teaching on the rapture and the teaching that Jesus could come back at any moment (the doctrine of immanency) for His church was taught by...

The Shepherd of Hermes in 150 AD

Victorenous, the Bishop of Gatow in 270 AD

Jerome in the Latin Vulgate in 400 AD

Reverend Dolacentoin 1600

Joseph Matty in 1627

Increase Matther in 1628

Peter Jarue in 1687

John Asgil in 1700

John Gil in 1748

James McKnight in 1763

Morgan Edwards in 1744

Thomas Scott in 1792

John Darby in 1820

John Darby didn't invent these teaching in 1820, there had been long line of men who held to this belief. Now as we continue, the next thing we need to understand is when will the rapture occur?

THE DATE WILL BE...

It will be on September 25th.... Just kidding! Jesus makes it very clear that the coming of the Lord will be sudden and without warning. (Matthew 25:13, Mark 13:35, 1 Thessalonians 5:2, 2 Peter 3:10) Every prediction we hear on TV or on the Internet comes and goes to no avail because again, we can have our opinions but God says what He means and means what He says. No one knows the day or the hour. When I say, "when will it be?" I mean in reference to the Great Tribulation.

There is coming on planet earth a time of great trouble. Called the time of Jacob's trouble in Jeremiah 30:7, Daniel's 70th Week from Daniel chapter 9 and the Great Tribulation in Matthew 24 and Revelation 2 and 7, this is going to be a time where the judgment of God is poured out on a Christ rejecting world. It will also be the time when the nation of Israel is woken up from her spiritual slumber and realizes Jesus was and is the Messiah. The question concerning the timing of the rapture is this; will it happen before, during or after the Great Tribulation? While not all Christians believe in the rapture, those that do believe it believe it will be one of those three options. Let's consider all three possibilities.

POST-TRIBULATION VIEW

Some believe the rapture of the church will happen at the very end of the tribulation period. This is because of the language in some of the rapture verses that speak of believers going through tribulation, and the mention of trumpets in both I Corinthians and I Thessalonians. In the book of Revelation there are seven trumpet judgments and so some tie the timing of the rapture with the blowing of the last trumpet toward the end of the Great Tribulation.

I personally do not hold to this belief because number one, I think there is a misunderstanding of terms like "elect" and "tribulation" in the scripture. Some who hold to the post-tribulation view quote verses like Matthew 24:21 that says, "For then there will be great tribulation, such as has not been since the beginning of the world until this time, no, nor ever shall be. And unless those days were shortened, no flesh would be saved; but for the elect's sake those days will be shortened."

"You see," they say, "'the elect go through the Great Tribulation." We get this idea since we think of "elect" people as referring to the church. The problem is "elect" is also a title for Israel. Isaiah 45:4 says, "For Jacob My servant's sake, And Israel My elect."

The same thing is true with the word, "saints". We see saints living on earth during the tribulation. (Revelation 13:7) How could there be a rapture of the church before the Tribulation period and yet saints are still on earth? Well just as with the word "elect", the Jewish people are also called "saints" in Deuteronomy 33:3 and 2 Chronicles 6:41, and also please don't forget I believe there will be Christians on earth during the tribulation period. I believe people who you have shared Jesus with, who do not know the Lord today, will get saved when the Antichrist is revealed and the world starts looking like you said it would. Just because we see "saints" and "elect" in the tribulation period does not mean God does not rapture His Church before the Great Tribulation begins.

Another misunderstood word is "tribulation." Jesus said in John 16:33, "In the world you shall have tribulation." Some see that as a promise from Jesus that believers will go through the Great Tribulation. However I believe Jesus is telling us in this life you shall have trouble, tribulation, but the specific, Great Tribulation is something I believe we need not go through.

Another thing people ask and wonder about is Matthew 24:31 which says, "And He will send His angels with a great sound of a trumpet, and they will gather together His elect from the four winds, from one end of heaven to the other." There it is right there. Jesus is speaking about an event at the end of the tribulation period. (I agree) There are trumpets and people being gathered. (I agree) So this is clearly a post tribulation rapture. (I do not agree)Jesus does return at the end of the Great Tribulation period. I see a difference between the rapture and the Second Coming of Jesus Christ as recorded in Revelation 19 and Matthew 24. When Jesus raptures the church, we will meet Him in the clouds and He will return to heaven with us. (I Thessalonians 4:13-18) When the second coming happens He will put a foot on the Mount of Olives and it will split in two and every eye will see Him and He will stay on earth and rule for 1,000 years. (Revelation 19-20) Matthew 24:31 in my opinion is a reference to the second coming of Jesus as He gathers and calls His people not just from the earth as will be the case in the rapture of the church, but from "one end of heaven to the other, " as it saying in Matthew 24:31.

Another confusing topic has to do with the trumpets. If Paul says the rapture will happen at the last trumpet, and there are trumpet judgments at the end of the tribulation, then this view makes sense. Something to understand however, is the trumpet judgments in Revelation 8 and 9 are trumpets being blown by angels. I Thessalonians 4:16 says that what is blown at the rapture is the "trump of God." There are only two times in the Bible the trump of God is mentioned. The first is in Exodus 19 when God blows a trumpet to call the nation of Israel as a nation under the laws of the Ten Commandments. In I Thessalonians 4 when God will blow His trumpet for the second time, this time to call the church to Himself. So there are only two trumps of God, the first trump, the last trump, and then of course there is Donald Trump but he doesn't count. The rapture will happen when God Himself blows His trumpet for the second and final time.

Another thing to keep in mind is although we read the phrase, "at the last trump" and because we are not familiar with that phrase, we start looking for connections to the seven trumpet judgments in the book of Revelation. That would not have been the understanding of the first century reader. Many Bible scholars see the "last trump" as a well-known idiom in the first century because of Roman warfare.

When Roman camp was to be broken up whether in the

middle of the night or in the day, a trumpet was sounded. The first blast signaled to them, "Strike the tents and prepare to depart." The second trumpet signaled, "Fall into line". When what was called "the last trump" sounded, it signaled that is was time to "March away". I believe Paul was using a familiar phrase everyone understood in the first century as God's sign to us as believers it was time to march away. There is no need to connect the "the last trump" with the seven trumpet judgments in the book of Revelation.

MID-TRIBULATION VIEW OR PRE-WRATH VIEW

Another belief concerning the rapture is the Mid-Tribulation view, the belief that the rapture will happen in the middle of the tribulation period. Those that hold to this belief see the second half of the tribulation as God pouring out His wrath on a Christ rejecting world whereas the first half will just be chaos on earth. In their belief the rapture happens before God's wrath starts pouring out on the world since as the church we are "not appointed to wrath." (I Thessalonians 5:9)

I do not personally hold to the pre-wrath position because when you study Revelation 6:16-17, which most scholars believe starts the tribulation period, the judgments are described there as the "wrath of the Lamb" and the "wrath of God." It is clear to me that God's wrath is being poured out on the world from the very beginning of the tribulation period.

Those that hold to a middle tribulation view of the rapture or even the end of the tribulation period for that matter, have to deal with the problem that Jesus said, "Watch therefore, for you know neither the day nor the hour in which the Son of Man is coming." (Matthew 25:13) You see, we are given exact timing for the Tribulation. We are told it is divided in into two, three and half-year periods of time. (Daniel 9) That each of those periods are exactly 42 months (Revelation 11:2, 13:5) and we even know the exact number of days, 1260 (Revelation 11:3, 12:6). It is like God goes out of His way to let you know the exact timing of the tribulation period. My point is if you believe the rapture will happen in the middle of the tribulation period then you start counting from the day the Antichrist is revealed (the official start of the tribulation period) and 1260 days later you will have the rapture. Or if you start counting in the middle at the Abomination of Desolation (Matthew 24:15) and go 1260 days to the end of the tribulation you come to the post tribulation rapture. Either way you now know the exact day of the rapture, which Jesus said you would not.

So to me, no matter how much it seems to be mocked in today's Christianity, I believe that Jesus will come back for His church before the tribulation even begins. I believe this not just because I personally have a few problems with some of the other theories concerning the rapture, but I also have 4 reasons I believe in the Pre- Tribulation rapture. We'll look at those in our final chapter.

FURTHER READING AND STUDY

"Things to come " by J. Dwight Pentecost – available through Amazon

"The Rapture Question" by John Walvoord – available through Amazon

"The Case for a pretribulational rapture" DVD by Charlie Campbe – avaiable on Alwaysbeready.com

13

Man
His Future (Part Two)

WHEN DOES THE RAPTURE HAPPEN?

"Then we who are alive and remain shall be caught up together with them in the clouds to meet the Lord in the air. And thus we shall always be with the Lord. Therefore comfort one another with these words.."

I Thessalonians 4:17-18

It's clear from our last chapter that I believe the rapture of the church will occur before the Great Tribulation. Here are my four reasons for my belief in a Pre-Tribulation rapture. Because I am still one of the few who love alliterations, each reason begins with the letter "P".

WHY I BELIEVE IN A PRE-TRIBULATION RAPTURE: PROMISE OF COMFORT

After explaining the rapture of the church, Paul says in I Thessalonians 4:18, "Therefore comfort one another with these words." In other words, the idea of the rapture of the church is supposed to be comforting. Paul says the same thing in I Thessalonians 5:11, and the author of Hebrews makes the same point in Hebrews 10:25. The idea of God coming back for His church was to be something that the church would comfort each other with. Now maybe it is just me but the idea of saying, "Hey you are going to be pounded by 100 pound hailstones, you are going to see the world torn apart but take comfort, it's only 7 years until we see Jesus!" is not very comforting. Even though trials and life gets more difficult as time goes on, to hear God is going to take us out before it gets really bad is a comfort. Before God starts judging sin, He is going to take us out of this place. To me, that is a great comfort.

Some accuse people like me of being an escapist, I just want to escape the tribulation period, and to that I say, 'You bet I do!' Isn't that what Jesus taught us to pray as well? Jesus said in Luke 21:36 after teaching about the tribulation period, "Watch therefore and pray always that you may be counted worthy to escape all these things that will come to pass and stand before the son of man." I don't want to escape life or ministry; I try to squeeze all I can out of every day, month and year God gives me to serve Him. Just ask my wife, who would love it if I would slow down. I don't want to get out of serving the Lord, but one day He will blow His trumpet and say to you and me, "come up here." (Revelation 4:1) Then we get to live in heaven with Him forever, not experiencing the Great Tribulation; that to me is comforting!

WHY I BELIEVE IN A PRE-TRIBULATION RAPTURE: PURPOSE OF THE TRIBULATION PERIOD

I in no way believe that Christians get out of hard times because we are Christians. I really believe the opposite is some-times true, however the tribulation period is different than just a hard time of trial. There are two main purposes for the Great Trib-ulation. The first purpose is to pour out God's wrath on a Christ rejecting world. Revelation 6 makes this clear. As God pours out seal judgments and trumpet judgments and bowl judgments, He is pouring out His wrath on a world that does not want Him to rule over them.

Now, as a believer, the wrath of God that I completely deserve has already been poured out on Jesus on the cross for me. I Thessalonians 5:9 says, "For God did not appoint us to wrath, but to obtain salvation through our Lord Jesus Christ." The first purpose of the tribulation is to pour out God's wrath on a Christ rejecting world. God's wrath was poured out on Jesus for you and me if you are Christian, therefore there is no need for you to go through the tribulation period.

The second purpose for the Great tribulation is to deal with the nation of Israel. In Daniel chapter 9, God tells Daniel that He is going to work with the nation of Israel for 490 years. 483 of those years took place from the command to go and restore and rebuild Jerusalem given by the Persian King Artaxerxes, to the time when Jesus walked into the city of Jerusalem on what we call today Palm Sunday. That time period was 483 years to the day. At that time, God's prophetic time clock with the Jews was put on hold as God began to work with a new group of people made up of Jews and Gentiles. We know this to be the church, and once the church is taken off the scene, there remains a seven-year period of work to be done. This is when God is going to be working directly with the nation of Israel. Since the church is not Israel and the wrath of God has already been poured out on Jesus for us on the cross, there remains no reason for the church to go through the tribulation period.

WHY I BELIEVE IN A PRE-TRIBULATION RAPTURE: PICTURES IN THE OLD TESTAMENT

I believe that in the true and historical stories in the Old Testament, God allowed there to be types or pictures of what He was going to do in the future. A few of these point to what God is going to do in the rapture of the church.

First, consider the Jewish wedding feast. Jewish weddings were much different than weddings today. The first thing that was considerably different was the bride-to-be didn't know when the wedding day would be. She was to just be ready for her groom to show up. Can you image that one ladies? The groom, after the engagement, would return to his father's house and begin building an addition on his father's house. The groom didn't know when the wedding would be either, for it was up to the father to examine the project and let the son known when everything was ready. Once the father gave the okay, the groom would come for his bride and they would begin a seven-day feast together with family and friends.

Now, consider that in light of what we know about Jesus coming for you and me as the church. First of all, we as the bride have no idea when Jesus is coming back. What has He been doing since He left earth in Luke 24? He has been preparing a place for you and me in His Father's house. Someday, I believe soon, the Father will give the okay and Jesus will come back for His bride. Not to then come right back down to earth in the second coming, as is the view of the Post- Tribulationist, but instead He will take His bride to a seven year wedding feast.

Another picture to consider is that of Lot in the book of Genesis. Lot was in the wicked city of Sodom and Gomorrah and God decided that city was going to be destroyed for its wickedness. Before God destroyed the city He had to get Lot out of that city. Abraham had already said that the Lord would not "slay the righteous with the wicked." (Genesis 18:25) When the angels came to Lot's house they told him, "I cannot do anything until you are safely out of the city." (Genesis 19:22) There seems to be a pattern of God removing His people out of a situation before His wrath is poured out.

The final picture I think is the best one, and it is the picture of Noah's flood. Some of you think, "Well I am glad you brought that up." Noah's flood, in your opinion, is the best picture of what

God is going to do in the Tribulation period because some of you believe that God is not going to rapture His people out of this world, but instead preserve them through like he did Noah. However, there are actually three different types of people in the Noah's flood story.

There was the world that perished, a picture of those who will go through the tribulation period. There is Noah and his family that were preserved through the flood and they are a picture of those Jews whom God will seal and preserve through the Great Tribulation period. (Revelation 7 &14). The final type in the Noah story is Enoch. Enoch I believe is a picture of the church for he was taken off the scene before the destruction of the flood ever began. (Genesis 5:24)

WHY I BELIEVE IN A PRE-TRIBULATION RAPTURE: THE PREACHING OF IMMANENCY

The final reason and my personal favorite is the fact that Jesus, Paul and Peter all preached the doctrine of immanency; that Jesus could return at any moment for His church. I will list just a few of the many examples. "Let your gentleness be known to all men, for the Lord is at hand." (Philippians 4:5) "Surely I am coming quickly." (Revelation 22:20) The clear preaching of the New Testament is to expect Jesus soon.

The only belief concerning the rapture that allows for the doctrine of immanency is the Pre-Tribulation rapture. For if you hold to the Post-tribulation view, then there are at least seven years between today and the coming of Jesus for His church. If you hold to the Mid-Tribulation or Pre-Wrath view, there are at least three and half years that have to transpire before the coming of the Lord for His church. Only the Pre-Tribulation rapture view allows for Jesus to come back for His church at any moment.

WHY DOES THE PRE TRIBULATION VIEW MATTER?

Why am I taking the last chapter of this book to deal with this subject? Well, as I said in chapter one, theology matters! What you believe about God and His Word will affect what you do and how you live. I believe this is no more true than with the rapture of the church. Not all believe this, of course. Pastor Rob Bell said, "The pre-tribulation rapture theory is one of the most devastating things the church has believed in the last hundred years. It has caused us to treat our planet without care." [1]

Now, that is just crazy to me. I believe Jesus could come back today for His church but that has never led me to throw trash out my car window. It has never led me to not want to live pure or serve the Lord effectively; in fact I believe it produces quite the opposite.

Consider Matthew 24:45-51, "Who then is a faithful and wise servant, whom his master made ruler over his household, to give them food in due season? Blessed is that servant whom his master, when he comes, will find so doing. Assuredly, I say to you that he will make him ruler over all his goods. But if that evil servant says in his heart, 'My master is delaying his coming,' and begins to beat his fellow servants, and to eat and drink with the drunkards, the master of that servant will come on a day when he is not looking for him and at an hour that he is not aware of, and will cut him in two and appoint him his portion with the hypocrites. There shall be weeping and gnashing of teeth."

Jesus says that expecting His soon return will affect my priorities. I can live anyway I want, but if I really believe Jesus could come back for me today, it would change the way I do almost everything. I think of my two girls. They have been to many weddings because I am a pastor. I watch them looking and evaluating the wedding, "Oh I like that dress, I like those decorations, oh, I wouldn't do that." They are planning for their future weddings but because they are at the time of this writing, 13 and 9, their wedding day is just a future dream. One day a long, long time from now, a young man will come along and ask for my daughter's hand in marriage.

Now, if he loves Jesus with all his heart and if he loves my daughter with all of his heart and if he is independently wealthy so Christy and I can retire (just kidding), then maybe I will say yes. At that moment, everything will change for my daughter that is getting married. The dream becomes a reality with a date. She will change the way she spends money, she will change the way she spends her time and some girls even change the way they eat. When I consider that Jesus could come for me today it should change how I spend my money, how I spend my time, how I live my life because what you believe effects how you live.

Expecting Jesus to come back at any moment affects the way I treat people. Look back at verse 48 and 49 of Matthew 24. The servant who says, 'My master is delaying His coming' has the tendency to treat other carelessly because they do not expect to see the master soon. My children can sometimes fight and bicker when I am not in the room or when they think I am not listening, but the minute I enter their presence the fighting stops because they know it is not appropriate behavior. I know I am supposed to love my fellow man. I know I am supposed to care for the poor and the orphans and the widows, and when I expect to see Jesus soon, that is actually far more likely to happen.

Expecting Jesus to come back soon also affects my purity. Jesus said in verse 49 of Matthew 24 that the servant who believes the Lord is delaying His coming begins to live impurely.

We know this to be the case. If you knew for sure the Lord was coming back tonight, would any of you pick today to get drunk, to be bitter, and to view pornography? No way, not if you think Jesus is coming tonight!

When I was 9 years old a book came out called, 88 Reasons Why Jesus is Coming Back in 1988. Now obviously, that was a silly book, but some I knew didn't think so, and started to give me the countdown. "3 months until Jesus comes back." "2 weeks until heaven." "'You are going to see God next week" and then "Today's the day." I remember going to school that day and I had no desire at all to sin. No desire to cheat, to be unkind, to talk back to my mom or teachers and the reason, because it just might be today that I saw Jesus face to face! Now, obviously writing such a book is never a good idea, but to think on the fact that today, I might see Jesus, I believe does wonders for your priorities and purity and passion to help hurting people and share Jesus with lost people.

REDEEMING THE TIME

To not live with the expectation of seeing Jesus soon has the potential to allow lots of wasted moments and opportunities in this life. I believe that is what Jesus is saying in Matthew 24:51. I do not believe Jesus is saying that if we do not live expecting

His soon return and it results in sinful living and poor treatment of others, we are not going to heaven. That would contradict so many other clear scriptures in the Word of God. We are not saved by our works, however I do believe we can lose out on reward for eternity because we choose to live our lives in brutality and carnality.

I believe for that reason, God wants every generation to expect His soon return for His church. Paul believed it, Spurgeon believed it, Moody believed it; Pastor Chuck Smith believed Jesus could come back at any moment. Now you might say, "Yeah those guys are all in heaven, so they were wrong. Jesus did not come back for His church in their lifetime." That, of course, is true, however if Jesus does not come back in our lifetime but we live each day living as if He might and we live a life of right priorities, purity and passion for people, would you be okay with that? I hope my life impacts people a small fraction of the amount that the lives of the likes of Paul the apostle, Spurgeon, Moody or Pastor Chuck effected people.

Again, it is not my heart to create division. I love my brothers and sister that have minor differences in what they believe about God, the process of salvation and the Lord's return. I love them and I appreciate their ministries and what they do for the kingdom of God. I simply believe that theology matters.

What you believe about God, salvation, and end times events will affect the way you worship, evangelize and live. For me, the beliefs that I hold dear have challenged me to trust a God that is greater than I ever pretend to be. It has challenged me to love the lost and care for the poor. It has challenged me to share my faith and live a life where holiness matters. Like you, I am far from perfect or sinless, but theology, what I believe about God, has laid a foundation for faith and growth and maturity in my life and I pray it does the same for you as well.

FURTHER READING AND STUDY

- "Things to come " by J. Dwight Pentecost – available through Amazon

- "The Rapture Question" by John Walvoord – available through Amazon

- "The Case for a pretribulational rapture" DVD by Charlie Campbe – avaiable on Alwaysbeready.com

About the Author

Jason Duff has been a serving as a fulltime minister since 1999 when he became the Youth Pastor at Calvary Chapel Vista, in Vista California. From 2004–2012 Jason served as the Senior Pastor of Calvary Chapel Paris, in Paris, Texas. In 2013 Jason rejoined the staff at Calvary Chapel Vista as a teaching pastor. Then in August of 2015 Jason became the Senior Pastor of the The Garden Fellowship in Bermuda Dunes, California. His online studies can be accessed at both calvaryvista.com under 'sermons,' and at thegardenfellowship.com. His podcast can be accessed through searching "jason duff" on i-tunes. Jason currently lives in Palm Desert, California with his wife Christy and three children Haley, Jonathan, and Aleah.

Booking Information

If you would like to inquire about having Pastor Jason teach at your church, retreat, camp, or conference, please send an email request to jasonduff7@gmail.com with the dates requested, theme or topic, retreat size, and location.

www.thegardenfellowship.com